THE WAR OF THE PRIEST HOOD

AN EXPOSITION OF
THE ARMOR OF GOD

ENDORSEMENTS

....

Be prepared for a substantive paradigm shift. In this book Uri Brito offers a sound Biblical interpretation of an all-too-commonly misunderstood and misapplied truth. In the process, he serves up a practical, inspiring, and refreshing vision of the calling of every gospel believer.

GEORGE GRANT
Pastor Emeritus, Parish Presbyterian Church (Franklin, TN)

We need the armor of God because Jesus deploys us to battle dragons and the Dragon. In *The War of the Priesthood*, Pastor Uri Brito shows that God has given us all we need, His own armor, a priestly panoply to take on principalities and powers. Combining keen pastoral and biblical insight, Pastor Brito identifies our gear and tells us how to use it. *The War of the Priesthood* is a challenging, inspiring field manual for spiritual warriors old and young.

PETER LEITHART
President, Theopolis Institute

You can find a man who is happy to be a king. And you can find a man who is happy to be a priest. But a sword-wielding priesthood? That's a rarer sight than spotting your local vegetarian down at the community barbeque festival. Nevertheless, from the time of Moses, our Lord promised that we would be a kingdom of priests. Uri is a faithful guide as the Church looks to the fulfillment of that promise. In this work, you have a potent passage of Scripture laid open, one that has much to teach the Christian Church today. The students who attended the New Saint Andrews CALLED conference were particularly blessed by this material, and I am sure you will be, too.

JARED LONGSHORE
Associate Pastor, Christ Church (Moscow, ID)

In our days of over-politicization within the culture and over-pietization within the Church, Dr. Uri Brito presents a biblical theology of spiritual warfare that encompasses the cosmos. In fact, this book is something of a mini-biblical theology. Dr. Brito weaves biblical, theological, historical, and pastoral truth to equip the ordinary Christian for the battles he faces daily. It is a battle the priesthood of the saints—behind Christ the cosmic Victor—will win.

P. ANDREW SANDLIN
Founder & President, Center for Cultural Leadership

THE
WAR
OF THE
PRIEST
HOOD

AN EXPOSITION OF
THE ARMOR OF GOD

URIESOU BRITO

NOGGINNOSE
PRESS

THE WAR OF THE PRIESTHOOD:
AN EXPOSITION OF THE ARMOR OF GOD

ISBN 978-1-956611-05-2

Edited by Rivers Houseal
Cover and interior design by Houseal Creative

———

Nogginnose Press
PO Box 96
Smithville, AR 72466 USA
nogginnose.com

*This book is dedicated to
the CALLED staff of
New Saint Andrews College
in Moscow, Idaho.*

CONTENTS

ACKNOWLEDGMENTS

....

When I preached through the Armor of God over five years ago, I had scattered notes about Roman gear and armament. But the further I dug into Paul's language, I concluded that Paul is rarely content to spread the supremacy of the Roman world to his readers.

Instead, Paul wished to ground much of his labors, theological insights, and metaphors in the language he knew so well: the Old Testament. He was a Hebrew of Hebrews (Philippians 3:5), which means his interpretive reality is shaped after Aaron's toes, beard, and head. The background music for Paul's writing is the liturgical psalms of God's people. For Paul to end an entire book by incorporating a Roman Empire metaphor would be disastrous and an unfortunate way to secure the Ephesians' trust in the Jewish Messiah.

These insights were gained through the careful interaction with the writings of my biblical mentor, James B. Jordan, with whom I served at Providence Church in Pensacola, Florida. His insights in books and lectures shaped me in more ways than I will ever truly know in this life. I suspect he may disagree with interpretive observations, especially my insistence on making the turban a sign of our baptismal identity. Yet, I am sure he would add an *amen* to my hermeneutical efforts.

Finally, I want to praise the CALLED conference team in Moscow, Idaho, for hosting me with such fervor. Their energy throughout the two weeks and consistent engagement with my lectures moved me. They sealed my interest in publishing this material in considerable measure because they set the stage for each of my talks on the armor of God, and incorporated over 300 students into the narrative of those talks day and night, in the lecture hall and the dormitory. I wish to offer a special gratitude to Caleb Salmon and Iain Anderson for organizing the week. I will not forget my time in July of 2023.

Uriesou Brito

INTRODUCTION

....

When our Jesus entered the scene of first-century Palestine, he entered it nakedly, as a babe sheltered by a manger. He humbled himself by dressing in human flesh for us and our salvation (Galatians 4:4). He was born of a virgin, fully dependent on motherly nurture, and trained in Israel's history and liturgy from his earliest days. Thus, he grew in wisdom, stature, and favor with God and man (Luke 2:52).

Jesus embodied the theology of Israel and Israel's God. The nurture and admonition he received built a particular disposition—a template for warfare against everything that opposed the worship of Yahweh. He was Israel's great defender; indeed, he was the true Israelite from the line of David. As the hymn-writer says, "David's Son, yet David's Lord."[1]

The God-Man matured for Israel's sake. For thirty years, he pursued righteousness, submitting to the laws of his forefathers in circumcision (Luke 2:21), celebrating the history of his people at Passover (Luke 2:41), and

....

1   Thomas Kelly, "Stricken, Smitten, and Afflicted," 1804.

following Joseph's profession as a carpenter (Matthew 13:55; Mark 6:3).

Now, he must be about his Father's business.

His cousin, John the Forerunner, comes from the desert to prepare the way for this catechized Israelite. To confirm his own calling as the ordained priest of Israel, Jesus was baptized by this greatest of all prophets (Luke 7:28). When he went into the water, the Spirit descended upon him like a dove, the heavens opened, and all Heavenly grace was poured on Israel's King. In baptism, Jesus put on royal clothing, with two royal witnesses affirming his call: the Father and the Spirit. The Triune God gathered for Israel's most noble ordination service.

Jesus' entire ceremonial and liturgical life prepared him for this event. He knew this calling was not to idleness in the academic ivory towers, but to something far greater. When Jesus received the Spirit, he embarked on a mission to protect Israel—even if Israel's enemies were the leaders charged with protecting Israel's God.

Jesus' first ordination task was clear: he charged the gates of Hell by overcoming Satan's temptations.

Israel's religion was corrupt because she embraced a new father (John 8:44). Therefore, Jesus went to the very root of evil. He embarked on a mission to defend true worship and protect Israel's liturgy and God from principalities and powers.

Jesus was led by the Spirit into the wilderness (Matthew 4:1). From his Lenten experience there, he learned the deceitful ways of the Evil One. The forty days of testing were a harsh pastoral internship. But his temptations gave him discernment to detect and test the spirits. His training provided the lenses to see the devil's ways and put into practice his theological and liturgical training in defense of his nation.

Jesus' response to the liturgy of evil was to return to Israel's catechism. Jesus did not doubt God's word, as the first Adam did. Instead, he reiterated God's Word by affirming his ordination vows.

The wilderness temptations provide the pattern for Jesus' new calling as the true priest: to fight the devil, and war against those ensnared by the devil, for three years.

Our Lord endured three temptations, a triad of evils that challenged the heart of his liturgical and theological training. The Gospel of Matthew provides a brief outline of these tests:

THE FIRST TEMPTATION

> **And the tempter came and said to him, "If you are the Son of God, command these stones to become loaves of bread."**
>
> MATTHEW 4:3

The Gospels connect the tempter of Genesis 3 to this tempter in Matthew 4. The Serpent of the first Garden comes to the Second Adam, Jesus Christ. He was able to deceive the first Adam. If the Devil defeats the Second Adam, he has won the battle.

The tempter addresses Jesus as the Son of God, in the likeness of the first Adam. He tempts our Lord as he did Adam: he tells Jesus what he must do to satisfy his deep hunger, re-echoing the words he spoke to Eve in the Garden (Genesis 3:5).

If Adam and Eve had continued to be faithful to Yahweh, eventually God would have given them access to the tree of the knowledge of good and evil—but it was not yet time. Instead, they needed to mature and grow in their faithfulness. Now the same temptation is offered to Jesus. The Devil knows it is not time for Jesus to turn stones into bread, but he will conquer Israel's true priest if he can persuade him to take his reward *now*.

Satan uses a clear contrast to entice our Lord. Biblically, stones symbolize death. We speak of stony hearts because they represent rebellion, and the Old Testament is replete with stones used as instruments of death. The Devil asks Jesus to transform a symbol of death into life. Bread is the antithesis of a stone; it refers to a living kingdom. The argument is quite appealing, since Jesus is called to be a priest unto life.

But Jesus is the *greater* Adam. He cannot succumb to the temptations as did his priestly predecessor. Jesus knows there is no ultimate good if he performs this transformation at this initial stage of his priestly work. The Devil is tempting him to fulfill his hunger now—yet

Jesus knows that he cannot seize the goodness of the kingdom until he gives his body as bread to the nations.

His response is the response that Adam and Eve failed to give in the garden:

> **"Man shall not live by bread alone, but by every word that comes from the mouth of God."** MATTHEW 4:4b

This quotation from Deuteronomy is not a rejection of bread, but an affirmation of his priestly calling to obey God before enjoying bread. In Jesus' mission, faithfulness precedes food. Jesus is the Suffering Servant, the beloved of the Father and the greater Isaac (Genesis 22), who knows that the cross comes first and glory after. Conformity to God's word demands that he fast so that later he may feast.

The Devil wishes to convince us that there are shortcuts to life and that there is another way to receive life than by trusting and obeying the Father's will—but Jesus overcomes this first devilish lie.

THE SECOND TEMPTATION

> **Then the Devil took him to the holy city and set him on the pinnacle of the temple...** MATTHEW 4:5

At the first temptation, Matthew speaks of "the tempter," but now he refers to "the Devil" as the one tempting Jesus.

The word devil is a generic word that means "slanderer." The Devil slanders God's people.

After failing the first time, the Devil takes Jesus to the holy city. This is an apparent reference to Jerusalem (Nehemiah 11:1). Matthew conveys something very particular when he refers to Jerusalem this way: the holy city is where God has chosen to put His name.

According to the text, Jesus is at the pinnacle of the temple—literally, the wing of the temple. The Devil twists the Scriptures to get his way, but at the same time, he does not *foolishly* twist the Scriptures. He is clearly familiar with them when he draws heavily from Psalm 91.

Psalm 91 is a psalm of comfort. It is a song that encourages God's people to find refuge and strength covered by God's wings. The reason the Devil takes Jesus to the wing of the temple is because he is playing on the wording of this psalm.

> **… And said to him, "If you are the Son of God, throw yourself down, for it is written, 'He will command his angels concerning you,' and 'On their hands they will bear you up, lest you strike your foot against a stone.'"** MATTHEW 4:6

He is saying: "Why don't you throw yourself, to prove that you are under the Father's wings and protection?" In other words, the reasoning goes, *What better place than the city of God to find refuge in God's care?*

But again, this is another way of tempting Jesus to do what he needs to do without enduring the tribulations ahead. Satan is provoking Jesus with generic biblical sentiments. "Receive the Father's protection now! Why endure the pain of the cross when the Father can take you under his wings and end this before it starts?"

The Devil's logic seems compelling. He has a biblical passage for what he wants Jesus to do, and the text he uses is true in what it claims. God protects His people when they are exiled and driven out of Egypt. He bears them up on eagle's wings and renews their strength (Isaiah 40:31). So, what is wrong with the Devil's statement?

The central problem with the Devil's view is to apply this promise without qualifications. He argues that you can throw yourself presumptuously, and the Father must protect you regardless.

But the guarantee of Psalm 91 is given to those who abide under the shadow of the Almighty; not to those who carelessly thrust themselves out from under his wings. The Psalmist calls us to hold fast to God's love and wait upon him. This is not an appeal to act independently of his care or to take matters into your own hands.

James Jordan observed:

> *It is one thing to be driven from the area of God's official wings, confident that He will extend His wings over you in exile. It is quite another to move out from under His wings*

*on your own, presumptuously counting on
His protection.*[2]

Jesus will be eventually driven out of the holy city. But he is not to force this. It will happen naturally, as part of his mission. When he is driven outside the gates, his Father will protect and raise him by removing the stone of death from the grave. Our Lord waits upon the LORD and receives protection from death in the resurrection from the dead.

> **Jesus said to him, "Again it is written, 'You shall not put the Lord your God to the test.'"** MATTHEW 4:7

If the Devil shows us how *not* to read the Scriptures, Jesus shows us how to read the Scriptures. Stanley Hauerwas writes:

> *Jesus is able to resist the devil, a devil able to quote scripture, by being a superior exegete to the one who would tempt him. Jesus, the faithful interpreter of Israel's scripture, teaches us how to read so that we might know how to resist the devil.*[3]

Jesus alludes to the people of Israel who doubted God's provision for them in the wilderness. In Exodus

....

2   James B. Jordan's lectures on Ephesians, wordmp3.com
3   Stanley Hauerwas, *Matthew* (Brazos, 2006), p. 50.

17, the people tested the Lord when they quarreled with Moses. They failed to believe that God would provide water at the right time. They wanted a God who could operate according to their needs and timing. The Israelites wished to domesticate God.

The Devil thought he would test Jesus as the people of Israel tested Yahweh. But again, Jesus knows that the Father will provide for his mission, and testing the Lord is just another way of saying, "I do not trust God to provide for me at the right time."

THE FINAL TEMPTATION

> **Again, the devil took him to a very high mountain and showed him all the kingdoms of the world and their glory. And he said to him, "All these I will give you, if you will fall down and worship me."**
>
> MATTHEW 4:8-9

The final temptation is the greatest because the Devil takes Jesus to an exceedingly high mountain.[4] Mountains play a significant role in Matthew's Gospel and are associated with worship. The fact that mountains are places of adoration fits well with the Devil's temptation: he wants Jesus to bow down and worship him.

....

4   Mountains are gardens; in Genesis, the four rivers flowed down. The Garden of Eden was on a mountain, elevated above any earthly realm.

The Devil shows him all the kingdoms of this world and their glory. He is tempting Jesus through the lust of the eyes. He is turning worship into something that can be consumed without God being the object of worship.

> **Then Jesus said to him, "Be gone, Satan! For it is written, "'You shall worship the Lord your God and him only shall you serve.'"** MATTHEW 4:10

This third temptation is connected to the other two. It takes a third rebuke for the Devil to get the point. Jesus answers the first temptation with timing: Jesus will become bread, and he will eat bread. He answers the second with timing, as well: he will throw himself under his Father's wings when his work is completed. Finally, Jesus states that the principle of worship is unchanged: there is only One true God worthy of all praise and adoration.

Indeed, Jesus will get everything—but the giver is not the Devil, but the Father. Psalm 110 promises that the nations will be given to Jesus as an inheritance. The deceiver wants Jesus to receive all things before the appointed time, but he fails. Our Lord knows that suffering precedes glory.

Jesus' forceful and powerful declaration concludes the wilderness temptations. It is crucial to see how Jesus defines his enemy. He does not say, "Be gone, Devil!" or "Be gone, Tempter!" Instead, he says: "Be gone, *Satan*!"

Satan means "adversary." This word can be used legally to speak of a prosecutor. Satan is the prosecutor who brings accusations against God and his people.

But here, the prosecutor sits down and quiets himself. He has nothing else to say. He has no more authority. He is shut up like the demons and the false teachers who stand up against the Anointed of God.

Jesus responds once more with a passage from Deuteronomy: "You shall worship the Lord your God and him only shall you serve" (Matthew 4:10). We are called to worship God with our heart, mind, soul, and strength. In the pursuit of righteousness, there can be no idolatry. Jesus established a principle for how to resist the devil. The result is that "...the devil left him, and behold, angels came and were ministering to him" (Matthew 4:11).

The Devil left him temporarily. He will reappear throughout the life of Jesus—even in his own disciples. But for now, there is a time of Sabbath rest. Jesus is baptized to war, and he has stood firm. Now he is refreshed for his earthly ministry.

A MINISTRY OF DISCERNMENT

The Devil's temptations in the wilderness provided discernment to fight other devils throughout Jesus' ministry.

The religious leaders are called to instruct God's people and train them in the language and law of God's word, but they led Israel to worship wrongly and to tempt the Lord our God. They are disguised servants of Satan.

Throughout his ministry, Jesus uses his discernment to chastise these teachers in Israel. He refers to them as blind guides (Luke 6:39), operating under the premises of the Father of lies (John 8:44). Jesus' ministry is to make all things new, but the religious leaders persist in transforming the fullness of worship into a desert place.

The lessons from the wilderness will accompany Jesus' labors throughout the Gospels. He is dressed in the armor of God, and he will see that armor attacked by the same leaders who are supposed to protect God's holy temple. But Jesus is the true priest dressed for war. He is prepared to live his baptismal life faithfully, with endurance. He sets his eyes on the mission and puts on the armor of God with boldness before the devil and his seed.

THE SATANIC
STRATEGIES

....

There is a powerful scene at the end of *Harry Potter & the Sorcerer's Stone* where Harry and the others fear uttering the name of the dark and evil nemesis. The wise Dumbledore rebukes Harry and says, "Call him Voldemort, Harry. Always use the proper name for things. Fear of a name increases fear of the thing itself."[5]

The fundamental reason why we fear the enemy is because we trust in our own garments. To our eyes, they are shiny, refined, and worldly attractive, but in the eyes of God, our self-created garments leave us exposed to the attacks of the evil one. We must understand why God dresses us in our baptismal attire; why it is better to be covered with something he gives us rather than to be covered with our own fig leaves. When our garments are not made by God, we will walk around timid, unprepared to name the enemy.

God's priests carry the name of Jesus wherever we go, because Jesus is our righteousness. He is the giver of

....

5   J.K. Rowling, *Harry Potter & the Sorcerer's Stone* (Scholastic, 1997).

all good gifts (James 1:17). Therefore, Christians can speak the name of Jesus boldly and speak out against the enemy who opposes our Lord's high-priesthood.

In the Bible, this enemy is known as the Accuser, the Serpent, the Devil, and many other titles. But the Church today operates in a hush-hush mode regarding the name of our archenemy. It may be that we are afraid to engage someone so dark, but it may also be a matter of ignorance. As a result, we don't know the Devil's strategies, art, or purpose on earth, and therefore we cannot accurately describe his schemes.

But there is another rationale for this failure: we do not utter his name because we do not think he invests himself in our destruction.

Therefore, we must offer an introduction to this dark, often-unnamed figure—and then establish the kind of war in which we are called to engage, and how we are to arm ourselves for it.

A DEVILISH BIOGRAPHY

The Bible says that everything God made was good.

Initially, this angel was good, but the prophetic books tell us that he fell. Ezekiel 28 gives us an inside look into the sin that turned him away from God's purposes forever.

> **Your heart was proud because of your beauty; you corrupted your wisdom for the sake of your splendor. I cast you to**

the ground; I exposed you before kings, to feast their eyes on you. EZEKIEL 28:17

Lucifer became so impressed with his own beauty, intelligence, power, and position that he began to desire for himself the honor and glory that belonged to God alone. The sin that corrupted Lucifer was self-generated pride.[6]

It was the same sin he used to tempt Adam and Eve in the garden. He urged them to fall as he did: "Become as gods and form your own kingdoms apart from the Creator!"

SATAN'S STRATEGIES

Satan has always been the enemy of God's people. In the Garden, Satan succeeded when he convinced our first parents to trust in their own ways. The curse meant the enemy could assemble an army to fight against the seed of the woman:

I will put enmity between you and the woman, and between your offspring and her offspring; he shall bruise your head, and you shall bruise his heel. GENESIS 3:15

This army is composed of all the offspring of Satan, those who would oppose the anointed of God. The

---

6   https://www.christianity.com/theology/theological-faq/how-did-lucifer-fall-and-become-satan-11557519.html

curse placed Satan's army in opposition to the seed of the woman, from Genesis 3:15 to Revelation 20.

In the end, Satan and his army are plunged into damnation. But until that day, there are many characteristics that his army displays in history. Those armed with God's armor must understand the strategies of Satan's army. I want to offer three of his main strategies:[7]

■ BEARING GOD'S NAME IN VAIN

Satan and his army specialize in lies.

They bear false witness as a way of life. This is clearly stated in John's Gospel when Jesus identifies the religious leaders as liars like their Father, the Devil (John 8:44). In Satan's family, the children turn out just like their Father: liars and deceivers. They absorb the habits of their liturgical guide and embrace his likeness.

From his earliest days, Satan tempted man to doubt the validity of God's word. "Did God really say…" The interaction Satan had with Adam and Eve intended to put every authority on the same plane. This strategy allows Satan to reinvent reality according to his own creed. He forms an alternative creation from which to derive meaning.

■ AGAINST THE KINGDOM

The Devil's second strategy is to fight against the kingdom.

....

7   See John M. Frame's *Systematic Theology*, (P&R Publishing, 2013) p. 775.

The prophet Daniel refers to Satan's army as seeking to take power over nations. This is why they are given this governmental title of "principalities and powers" in the Apostle Paul's letter to the Ephesians. Paul also refers to Satan as the "ruler of this world" (2 Corinthians 4:4). The title is apt for his rule before the arrival of Jesus.

Before the First Coming of Jesus, the world dwelt in the darkness of 400 years of silence. Satan's rule over the Old Covenant era and the interim history kept the Church silent. When Jesus enters history in human flesh, he interrupts the tyranny of silence and restores the voices of God's people.

But the Devil is still seeking whom he may devour, even in this present age.

The seed of the Serpent seeks to destroy the kingdom of God. Satan seeks to devour God's people by removing their ability to voice their loyalty to the Lord. This forms the basis for Satan's first encounter with Jesus in the wilderness.

It was no accident that the Holy Spirit led Jesus to confront evil as soon as he was ordained into his priestly role at baptism. Satan's words carried the day in the Old Covenant era when priests, kings, and prophets were deceived by his offers, but when Satan tempted Jesus, our Lord did not keep silent. Jesus is the greater priest, king, and prophet in whom there is no darkness at all (1 John 1:5). He answers with the voice of Heaven by claiming authority from God himself.

■ ACCUSING THE SAINTS

One of Satan's most-used strategies is to accuse the saints.

The name *Devil* means "slanderer" and "accuser." He constantly mocks Jesus and his army by taking the side of evil rulers, possessing image-bearers, causing havoc, and bringing chaos to the land. He seeks whom he may devour (1 Peter 5:8) by engaging our appetites and drawing us to use them sinfully.

Satan knows how to turn something good, like food, into something abused. He says, "Love food, but love it so much that it consumes you." That is the logic of the Accuser. He takes the thing that is good and transforms it into a source of frustration and pain.

C.S. Lewis capably describes the wiles of the evil one in *The Screwtape Letters*:

> Indeed the safest road to Hell is the gradual
> one—the gentle slope, soft underfoot,
> without sudden turnings, without milestones,
> without signposts.[8]

Satan lies, wars against the kingdom, and accuses God's people. If he can succeed in these endeavors, he has disrobed our priestly calling at some level.

This is a brief overview of Satan's life and strategies, but we must go further. We must speak of Satan's status.

....

8   C.S. Lewis, *The Screwtape Letters* (Geoffrey Bles, 1942).

The Christian must define the enemy accurately. We must not fear to speak his name, but we must also avoid the ditch of exalting the authority of Satan so much that we fail to see the work of Jesus in destroying and putting an ultimate end to Satan's agenda.

THE ESCHATOLOGY
OF EVIL

....

Istory is a story of stones thrown, heads crushed, rocky walls fallen, and temples rebuilt. Stones everywhere! Precious stones, colorful stones, blood-stained stones, and sparkling stones. The Bible plays out this theme in the context of life and death. Stones form the background of the Old Testament. Satan's descendants get crushed, and they rise again to tempt God's people. He sits around like a roaring lion, taking beating after beating. When will he die? When will he find his eternal end?

There are four stages to describe the ultimate death of Satan and his offspring. These help lay out a chronology of the operations of Satan throughout biblical history.

THE CHRONOLOGY OF SATAN'S DEFEAT

■ HISTORICAL DEFEATS

The first stage of Satan's demise is his historical defeats throughout the Old Testament. False teachers, false prophets, false gods, and false gospels are all examples of the serpent's defeats.

There is a conflict between two houses: a house of righteousness for the seed of the woman and a house of unrighteousness for the serpent's seed. When we read the Old Testament narratives, we may get the impression that the house of unrighteousness has the last laugh. But the joke is on him, and he is the defeated house because, in God's economy, righteousness only needs one smooth stone to defeat unrighteousness.

So, if famine or sword is against us, nothing can separate us from the love of God, which is in Christ Jesus. They may try to tie us up and cut out our glory, but in the end, he who sits in the heavens laughs. The Lord holds them in derision (Psalm 2).

He will raise ambassadors to defend his Name and his house. Biblical history testifies to the devil's defeat in the stories of Joseph, Samson, and David. There are stories that appear to vindicate the serpent's offspring, but ultimately, they all end with God's purposes established, because what men meant for evil, God meant for good (Genesis 50:20).

■ CRUSHED AT THE CROSS

The second stage of Satan's great defeat occurs on the cross, when the evil tyrant is crushed. The cross was the instrument of bodily death to Jesus, but also of damnation to the devil. The Father raised Jesus from the dead in a glorified body, but when the devil was crushed at the cross, there was no resurrection for him.

Hebrews says that Christ died, "that through death he might destroy the one who has the power of death, that is, the devil" (Hebrews 2:14). The cross was the place of victory for Jesus and the seed of the woman. Jesus stood tall with the Father's approval and stepped on the serpent's skull.

■ TO THE ENDS OF THE EARTH

The third stage of Satan's defeat comes through the labors of the Church in the Great Commission (Matthew 28:18-20).

The Lord's commission to his disciples marks a great reversal in history. We could already see types of this reversal: on the day Samson died, 3,000 enemies died too (Judges 16:27). The Egyptian armies, which symbolized Satan's offspring, died in the waters, persecuting God's people, and God's people were saved through the waters of baptism (1 Corinthians 10:1-2). Babel was dispersed in Genesis 6, but now Babel is subverted on Pentecost, and there were 3,000 friends baptized. Every conceivable curse laid upon God's people is beginning to be undone by the Church's work.

The history of the Church from Pentecost until the final coming of Jesus is a season of great reformation and renewal in the world. God is creating a holy nation, a royal priesthood, to go to the ends of the earth to share his gifts. Satan cannot stop the movement of the gospel from transforming every nation on the earth. He does not have the power or authority to stop Bible translations, missionaries, worship, and celebration from going to the ends of the earth.

The Church of the New Covenant is far superior to the Church of the Old Covenant, because we have a Spirit-inspired mission sealed by the death, resurrection, and ascension of Jesus. We move forth, crippling Satan's kingdom and houses, taking his possessions and beautifying our own. As Paul says, "When he ascended on high he led a host of captives, and he gave gifts to men" (Ephesians 4:8).

Luther's great hymn states:

> *And though this world, with devils filled,*
> *Should threaten to undo us,*
> *We will not fear, for God has willed*
> *His truth to triumph through us.*[9]

The truth is triumphing through the Church and her mission. She is paralyzing the gates of Hell, and the gates of Hell cannot prevail against her (Matthew 16:18-19).

But there is one final stage, which will be the culmination of all Satan's defeats. There is a time when the nations will roar in adoration for the ultimate head-crusher. On that day, they will rejoice without fearing

---

9   Martin Luther, "A Mighty Fortress Is Our God," 1529.

further intervention or conspiracy from the prince of darkness.

THE DEVIL'S FINAL DEFEAT

The final stage of Satan and his offspring comes at the end of the millennium. The Bible signals three sequential events at this end of history, described most clearly in Revelation 20. The focus is on the trajectory that leads to the termination of Satan and all his works.

> **Then I saw an angel coming down from heaven, holding in his hand the key to the bottomless pit and a great chain. And he seized the dragon, that ancient serpent, who is the devil and Satan, and bound him for a thousand years, and threw him into the pit, and shut it and sealed it over him, so that he might not deceive the nations any longer, until the thousand years were ended.** REVELATION 20:1-3a

Revelation describes the Devil as one descending from misery to misery. The text says that an angel comes down from Heaven, and he has the key to death and Hell. This messenger coming from Heaven is Jesus, who has the power to bind in Heaven and on earth. What does he do? He seizes the dragon, who is the devil and Satan. He binds him for a thousand years.

This becomes puzzling if someone believes this reference to a thousand years is still in the future. If this interpretation follows, they affirm that Satan is loose now and remains the god of this world until the end of history. But the New Testament shows that Satan was defeated at the cross in Hebrews 2, that Satan was bound in Matthew 12, and that death and evil were defeated at the resurrection in 1 Corinthians 15. Jesus' first coming and his eventual ascension dethroned the principalities and powers. He ascends to the highest Heaven as the true God of all creation.

John says that Satan was bound for a thousand years, which is symbolic of an extended period of time. In this case, the 1,000 years span from the first coming of Jesus in the first century to the final coming of Jesus at the end of history. John uses numbers to convey all sorts of realities, often rooted in Old Testament language. In Revelation 20, John uses the number 1,000 to refer to fullness or immensity (e.g. Psalm 84:10; Job 9:3; 1 Chronicles 16:15). One would be hard-pressed to take the number 1,000 literally in the most symbolic book of the Bible.

Revelation says that during the post-Pentecost era of history, the devil was bound but also thrown into the pit. He is shut in, and the pit is sealed over him so that he might not deceive the nations any longer until the thousand years were ended. Notice the trajectory of John's description: the angel comes down, binds the devil, throws him into the pit, shuts it, and seals it over him. Satan goes down, but not immediately to his fiery end. He is in a pit. He will stay there for a thousand years. His imprisonment began with the death of Jesus and was sealed when our Lord ascended to the right hand of the Father.

But what does that mean practically for the Church in our day? It means that the devil cannot keep the gospel from going to the ends of the earth: "…so that he might not deceive the nations any longer, until the thousand years were ended" (see Revelation 20:3).

The Serpent's head was crushed at the cross, and in the labors of the Church. He is in the place of death right now, but he is not entirely destroyed. The Bible is more layered and developed in its historical layout than that. Satan is crushed in multiple ways, so that his power is incrementally diminished.

In the Old Testament, with few exceptions, the gospel remained with one special people, Israel. There were hints that it would go to the ends of the earth in Samson, Jonah, and the prophets. But the Devil kept the nations in bondage, blinded, and so they remained lost.

In Revelation 20, the promise is that in the coming of Jesus—the beginning of the thousand-year reign—the nations would no longer be deceived.

Augustine writes:

> *The binding of the devil is his being*
> *prevented from the exercise of his whole*

> *power to seduce men, or fraudulently deceive*
> *them into taking part with him.*[10]

Ask the question, "Where is the devil now?" The answer is, "He is in a pit." He blinded the nations throughout the Old Testament; now, he is the one blinded by the darkness of the pit. He is disoriented and discombobulated. He does not have the same power he had before. He watches the nations coming to Jesus, and he groans in disgust. Yes, he still is active, but at a very limited capacity. He is like a vicious dog bound and eager to destroy, but he can't. He has his demons to do his bidding, but he knows his time is short.

The final theme is key in Revelation 20. According to John, Satan is released at the end of history for his final humiliation.

> **After that he must be released for a little while ... And when the thousand years are ended, Satan will be released from his prison and will come out to deceive the nations that are at the four corners of the earth ...** REVELATION 20:3b,7-8

The word used for Satan's release is *luthesetai*, which is in the passive. The idea is not that the Serpent found a hidden key in the pit and escaped, but rather that God was

---

10 Augustine, *City of God*, Book XX, Chapter 9.

the one who let him go. The purpose of this last episode of human history is to put on a show.

Throughout history, God's servants and martyrs have been used to entertain the wicked. Remember Samson, Jesus, Polycarp, Pothinus, and others humiliated before death? Now, in this last scene in world history, Satan is the one who comes out of the pit and becomes the freak show for the Church's entertainment.

Satan does gather pockets of rebels across the world—what Peter Leithart calls a "false Israel"[11]—for one more show. But that spectacle is short-lived:

> **And they marched up over the broad plain of the earth and surrounded the camp of the saints and the beloved city, but fire came down from heaven and consumed them, and the devil who had deceived them was thrown into the lake of fire and sulfur where the beast and the false prophet were, and they will be tormented day and night forever and ever.** REVELATION 20:9-10

Satan's cause is overthrown once and for all. Now he goes down, down, down to a ring of fire and his humiliation is complete. The text gives the distinct impression that this is not the kind of show that lasted

---

11 Peter J. Leithart's commentary on *Revelation*, (T&T Clark, 2018) p. 328.

very long; but it was enough to see the Serpent's final scheme against the people of God.

It failed because the Serpent had lost his grasp on reality. He was historically blind, fatally flawed, and culturally devastated. Until he is released at the end of history, all Satan can do is watch the Church, the city of God, win! The gospel goes to the ends of the earth!

At the end of history, we will look into a civilization that is largely Christianized. Yes, there will be rebels who will find refuge in false religion, but they will be overwhelmed by the Spirit-blessed gospel. In those final days of history, Christ will have dominion. Cultures, malls, pubs, grocery stores, churches, places of political power, art, architecture, and everything else will be Christianized.

When Satan is released, he will see a world where his efforts have failed, his deception is no longer effective, and his power is depleted. Then, Christ and all the lionhearted men of early and late Christendom will rise to watch the devil, his works, and his companions be tormented for all eternity in a lake of fire.

Human history begins with a promise in Genesis 3:15 that the seed of the woman shall crush the head of the Serpent. Then, the heads of serpents are crushed again and again. Then, Christ crushes the devil on the cross and history testifies to the devil's defeat and bondage. Then, the Church watches the humiliation of the Old Serpent one final time at the end of history.

The Church rejoices now that the Serpent is bound, blinded in a pit. But don't worry: there is more rejoicing to come when the Serpent suffers his final blow and the great head-crusher, Jesus Christ, receives the nations as his inheritance.

THE DEVIL'S CURRENT STATUS

So where does Satan stand now?

Jesus changed the effectiveness of Satan's labors. In his appearance to the nations, Jesus took the role of "ruler of the nations" from Satan. He accomplished this through his life, death, resurrection, and ascension. He took away Satan's power to deceive the nations (Revelation 20:3) and Satan can no longer restrict the gospel to a piece of land. When Jesus was manifested to the nations, the gospel went to the ends of the earth. Satan and his army no longer have the free range they had in the Old Covenant.

Satan's present status should compel us to think appropriately about his strategies. We are no longer expecting a suitable warrior to confront Satan. In Christ, we have justification through his resurrection (Romans 4:25), and his ascension vindicates his earthly claims to be ruler over all, including Satan himself.

THE CHURCH'S PRESENT POSTURE

The portrait of Satan's status provides biblical data for the Church's twofold posture of caution and confidence. Peter gives us this moderated approach:

> **Be sober-minded; be watchful. Your adversary the devil prowls around like a roaring lion, seeking someone to devour. Resist him, firm in your faith...**
>
> 1 PETER 5:8-9

Satan is defeated, awaiting his final judgment, but still harming. His end has not yet come; therefore, Christians need to be sober, vigilant, and aware of the strategies of the evil one. We must put on the armor of God with courage, for the days are evil.

If Satan is involved in a strategy against the royal priesthood, it is reasonable to assert that we are at war with him and his seed. The Church needs to develop its own strategy. She cannot stand aloof while Satan acts with intentionality to destroy her, as he has for all of human history. We must walk steadfastly in faith knowing that our confidence comes from the Lord of glory, who conquered death and Hell.

Satan's status and his sure end offer us a clear picture of who we are up against in history. Now, with caution, but also with sure confidence, we can see how Christ prepares us to face the schemes of the wicked one with his priestly armor.

THE CALL
TO COURAGE

....

As we enter into the description of the armor of God, we need to consider the context from which Paul builds this famous passage. It is clear from the opening language that Paul is reaching a proper conclusion to his entire argument:

> **Finally, be strong in the Lord and in the strength of his might.** EPHESIANS 6:10

Paul begins this section with this master statement, and verses 11-18 will amplify it.

The call to strength and might is not new in Paul's letter to the Ephesians. The previous chapter elaborates on what it means to be strong and mighty. Paul, the practical theologian, makes the case that when wives submit to their husbands (5:22), and husbands love their wives (5:25), and children obey their parents (6:1), and fathers do not provoke their children (6:4), they are strong in the might of their Lord. These practical relationship dynamics testify to the strength of the believer.

The beauty of the gospel is centered on the authority and power of Jesus. Our strength does not depend on forces that are depleted on a bad day or philosophies that go out of style in a decade. Instead, our strength is derived from Christ who is the same yesterday, today and forever (Hebrews 13:8).

When we walk by grace through faith, we are seated with Christ in the Heavenly places (Ephesians 2:6). Paul even compares the power given to the Church as the same power exerted by the Father when he raised Jesus from the dead and seated him at his right hand (1:18-21). All things come from him and through him. True strength is Christ-saturated strength!

John Calvin referred to this exhortation as a "summon to courage."[12] We are called to walk according to the Spirit, even as Christ walked before us (5:2). We are in Jesus, and the strength of Jesus is given to us as we march by faith. But the Apostle Paul is not done with his summons: he adds once more that we are to be strong *in the strength of his might*. It appears redundant, but Paul is adding a different component to his sermon.

He is being proverbial. In Proverbs, Solomon uses a method called Hebrew parallelism. It uses language to convey the same idea in two different ways. It adds emphasis to the command or proverb.

....

12   John Calvin's commentary on *Ephesians* (Grand Rapids, MI: Baker Books), p. 334.

Paul builds upon the first line by adding that our strength alone is insufficient. The source of our strength is the one who redeems us and grants us a new identity. We are lost if we find our strength to be the all in all of our walk. Our insufficiencies will quickly cause the armor of God to decay and corrupt. Our armor is secured and protected by the one whose right hand is mighty to save.

The Christian's courage and strength wars against the schemes of Satan. Satan lies, mocks, and seeks to destroy God's kingdom. Therefore, we must be strengthened to war for truth, righteousness, and the kingdom. Satan knows the crucial targets. He inspected the holy places and found the weaknesses of our faith. Now, we must uphold and defend the faith once and for all delivered to us (Jude 1:3).

THE ARENA OF TRUTH

The defense of truth is fundamental in the armor structure, as we will see. But Paul prefaces the attire's description by stressing our need for strength in the Lord. The arena of truth is the place persistently threatened by Satan.

This is precisely why Paul has already listed an array of behaviors that ought to characterize the Christian. These ethical themes preserve truth inside the body Christ gave himself to save (Ephesians 5:25). He begins with unified relationships in Ephesians 1-2, then spiritual maturity in chapters 3-4, and sacrificial living for the sake of husbands, wives, and children in chapter 5.

There are no "shortcuts to the spiritual … but there is also no mystery to it."[13] We do not have to stand around trying to figure out, *What is truth? What is the kingdom? What is righteousness?* A Christian is only confused about these things if they simply refuse to look or seek—or if they believe this is not really a war.

To deny that the Christian lives in constant warfare against evil, sin, and the Devil is to deny the gospel, because the gospel assumes that we are in constant war against the world, the flesh, and the Devil.

We uphold and defend truth in how we live and articulate what God says. None of us willingly say, "I have no interest in truth." But this is where what we say is contradicted by our day-to-day missed opportunities.

How often have we told ourselves, "I should have said something …" We often fail to uphold the truth by remaining silent. There is a fundamental problem if those around you do not know your faith and commitment to Christian truth. When the people around you are comfortable misrepresenting and mocking Jesus, something is wrong.

We will elaborate on this, but every concept of truth is being challenged today: sexuality, gender, marriage, purity, the authority of the Bible, etc. The opportunities

....

13   Bryan Chapell's commentary on *Ephesians* (P&R Publishing, 2009), p. 329.

for speaking truth are more abundant in our culture, because falsehood is pervasively articulated.

IN DEFENSE OF THE KINGDOM

Another area where we are called to pursue war is in defense of the kingdom. The strength of his might is the sanctifying power to fortify the kingdom of God. We have a confirmation of this premise in Jesus' words that the gates of Hell shall not prevail against the Church (Matthew 16:18).

When we read such a statement, we think that surely Hell is always attacking the people of God—but the text implies that the Church is always on the offensive, not sitting passively taking hits from the enemy.

We are strong in the Lord; therefore, we must be at the forefront of this warfare, not waiting to be attacked. The kingdom of God, especially the Church and the family, must be protected, fortified, and equipped to go forth courageously in the Name of Jesus.

THE RIGHTEOUS KINGDOM

Finally, we are to war for righteousness. The war for righteousness is the war for right living.

There is no greater liberty than setting your mind to the war ahead of you. If every morning we woke up praying, "Deliver us from evil, and lead us not into temptation," our mindset would be different in how we faced the day. But often we pray, "Deliver me from this deadline," or, "Lead me into prosperity."

Our warfare must begin with individual government. Everything flows from that. Righteousness is the rhythm that drives the kingdom of truth. This is why Paul offers a rich perspective on human relationships, and it is what differentiates the sons of God from the sons of disobedience (Ephesians 2:1-10).

Satan, of course, sets his trajectory against truth, the kingdom, and right living, which is why he will set his gaze towards you.

Fear of a name increases fear of the thing itself. Do not fear. His name is Satan. Be cautious, and be confident. Be strong in the Lord and the strength of his might. Live as baptized saints who wear God's kingdom armor wherever you go.

THE ARMOR
IMPERATIVE

....

Have you ever met someone who always wants immediate results? Quick weight loss, easy money, and fast food? These types of people represent a society eager to consume the next thing without savoring it. They take their journey with their eyes closed, only stopping to replenish their wants and then moving on to the next thing. They prefer to stay in the car, scrolling the quick array of Instagram reels while everyone else exits the vehicle and enjoys the sceneries, smells the environment, and captures the experience.

While life provides opportunities both to savor and to move fast, we instinctively know that those who taste and see in a particular way are bound for glory (Psalm 34:8). This is because they reflect most clearly the covenantal model of the Scriptures. Practically, they don't make plans only for the next day, but are people who know the times (1 Chronicles 12:32), setting the stage for the next forty years. They are the savorers of time because they are content to see little fruit now, so that they can reap a great harvest down the road. Whether they are alive or dead, the plan is generational—which is to say, covenantal.

The type of person worth emulating is the one who lives for the future while experiencing present joy. This means he fights for the *right* future; not just any future, but one rooted in truth and righteousness.

James B. Jordan notes in one of his essays that Satan "is willing to wait in the confidence that the next generation will be his."[14] Satan is a fallen angelic being who took his fall as a model for doing business on earth. Since he fell, everyone must fall with him, and like him.

Satan argues with Adam and Eve in the Garden that patience is not a virtue. So, he encourages them to follow in his train. He encourages them to eat the fruit and gain knowledge of good and evil *now*, be like gods *now*, take charge *now*, and receive glory *now*. This is the paradigm of the fall.

But Satan learned his lesson after the curse (Genesis 3:15). Throughout history, he has been patiently roaming around like a roaring lion. He is strategic. Where do you think he learned to strategize? From God himself.

God is always a perfect strategic genius. His ways are higher than our ways and his plans are perfectly executed at the right timing. God orchestrates his timing for our good, but Satan takes that patient strategy and carefully

14   James B. Jordan, "Old Rite Essays," wordmp3.com

waits to deceive Christians, to convince men and women to taste things before the right time.

Satan is real. Beyond that, he is patient. Satan uses his patience to his advantage. He counts on your impatience. His end goal is not a fast-food meal; it is a banquet filled with the souls of apathetic saints.

Satan's strategy is to deceive you into thinking that truth is irrelevant, the kingdom is not worth fighting for, and right living is a choice. If he can slowly guide you to that point where these things no longer matter to you—or perhaps they matter little—then he will be content. What then should be our response?

Our response is to play the patience game also. We need to understand Satan's strategies, and prepare for the long game.

THE STRATEGIES OF THE PRINCIPALITIES AND POWERS

In the book of Ephesians, Paul does not leave us wondering what to do.

He is very precise about the warfare in which you are supposed to engage. This is not a blogging or Twitter war; it is a death and blood and shouting and loving and singing and preaching and eucharist kind of war. By God's grace, we may never take up arms to fight, as was common in Israel's history, but we take up a new kind of war where we stand clearly against a culture guided by evil schemes.

So, Paul continues:

Finally, be strong in the Lord and in the strength of his might. Put on the whole armor of God, that you may be able to stand against the schemes of the devil.

EPHESIANS 6:10-11

When you hear this text, consider a few modern-day allurements. Consider the accessibility the Internet provides, with "sexual temptation, material indulgence, gambling, personal disengagement, and ungodly communication within a mouse-click of persons of every age and social station."[15] That is just the beginning.

We live in an age when, even if families sit together for a meal, every person engages in self-amusement. We don't sit to talk anymore. We don't get together with friends. Marriages are becoming functional, rather than divine stories of grace. We don't discuss good books or music; we are shaped by quick Instagram reels and TikTok celebrities.

These are all symptoms that we live in a culturally devastated environment—which is why we need to understand the Devil's schemes.

The solution is found in the Bible, in a three-fold outline:[16] we need to learn to speak the truth, fight for the kingdom, and live rightly in the sight of God and man.

....

15 Bryan Chapell's commentary on *Ephesians* (P&R Publishing, 2009), p. 328
16 John M. Frame's *Systematic Theology* outlines this model, though I have added considerably.

In short, we need to dress up for the occasion, and march to a different tune—the tune of angels, rather than masqueraded demons. This means the courage to say "Satan"—to say the name of the one who embodies evil. If fear of a name increases fear of the thing itself, then we need to say the name of our enemy and war against our fears.

THE COMPLETE ARMOR

Paul's imperative is clear: put on the armor.

For what purpose? To stand against the Devil. But what about the Devil must we stand against? His schemes. We could also refer to his maneuvers, traps, or tricks. Paul uses the language that was common in Israel's songs. The Psalm writers constantly warned against those who sought to entrap God's people devising wicked schemes for their destruction.[17]

When people ask, "Why are churches losing their stamina in the fight against evil?" my first reaction is to ask about their music repertoire on Sundays.

You know a lot about a church from what they sing. The more the Church sings robust psalms and hymns, the more she is exposed to good theology, good melodies, and biblical history. You will be better equipped to know your place in history and the war around you if you know

....

17   See Psalms 10:2, 21:11, 26:10, 37:7, 56:5, 119:150.

how God thinks about the world, and what songs are needed in each stage of your life.

We fight evil by singing to one another with psalms, hymns, and spiritual songs (Ephesians 5:19). We stand boldly against the schemes of the devil by raising our voices to the God of Israel.

The Apostle knew what was at stake at Ephesus. He wrote the book of Ephesians in an environment where wars and rumors of wars were constant, where there were temptations to revolt against authority and dishonor those they loved. Paul is not talking out of ignorance, but intimate experience.

Paul also saw a war behind the war—the spiritual war behind the physical wars. The spiritual and invisible wars are the genesis of all wars. Paul says that war is our present reality, and you need eyes to see it. Many blind themselves to see the war around us because they refuse to stand firm for truth, righteousness, and the kingdom of God.

This lesson is particularly poignant to younger Christians bombarded by wicked schemes. The decisions you make at this point in your lives will have a tremendous impact on shaping the kind of person you will be one day. Whether with social media, devotional life, piety, or peer interaction, these actions and reactions will shape you into something.

The end result of doing, thinking, and absorbing the evil culture around you is that you walk around oblivious of the warfare around you.

Paul offers an imperative: "Put on." The whole armor must be put on when you awaken. It is the first part of your daily ritual. Paul's case is that the armor is already yours, but you must renew it as you renew your minds and hearts.

Practically, this could be a call for reading, meditating, serving, or listening to the truth in the Scriptures. This could be through good theological and practical podcasts or book studies, praying with one another, studying together, or engaging in meaningful discussions.

These actions build courage and strength against the schemes of Satan. He lies, mocks, and seeks to destroy God's kingdom. Therefore, the armor of God is the kind of clothing that requires your body and soul to dress up for the occasion.

> **For we do not wrestle against flesh and blood, but against the rulers, against the authorities, against the cosmic powers over this present darkness, against the spiritual forces of evil in the heavenly places.** EPHESIANS 6:12

In the 16th century, one of Martin Luther's disciples, Thomas Muntzer, decided to take matters into his own hands.[18] He attempted to use military action to restore the world to the reality he believed should prevail. It is said that he used this text in Ephesians as a call to take up arms and do what Luther could not.

Luther quickly chastised Thomas by making the point that the appropriate weapons for warfare against principalities and powers are faith, the Word of God, baptism, and the Lord's Supper. These are things that come from Heaven.

Bryan Chapell writes, "Ours is not a magic religion full of mysterious incantations, secret handshakes, and arcane codes."[19] We have basic weapons, and these tools have proven fruitful for 2,000 years and will continue to bear fruit for the next 2,000 years. The Word, faith, and the sacraments of bread and wine and baptism are the ordinary preparation tools that God has given us. This is the ordinary way of growing in the gospel and weaning ourselves from ungodly habits.

We are fundamentally different from those who deny the gospel. We were dead in our trespasses and sins and now are alive together in Christ (Ephesians 2:5). We were aliens, but now are counted as household members. We were objects of wrath, but now are fellow citizens (2:12-13,19). We have a new pattern of living, walking in step with the Spirit (Galatians 5:25).

....

18   See *Christianity Through the Centuries* by Earle E. Cairn for a more thorough account.
19   Bryan Chapell's commentary on *Ephesians* (P&R Publishing, 2009), p. 330.

But the spiritual forces of evil come at us slowly, patiently, and generationally, because they understand the long-term strategy of warfare.

Those created for good works should grasp the importance of long-term preparation in the spheres of Church, home, and state. We may not see much fruit in this life, but the thousands of moments of investment—kisses, hugs, encouragement, and perseverance—will bear fruit in this life, whether you are alive to see it or not.

We war with the future in mind. We war as if we can see the glory of the future now—and indeed, by faith, Jesus already strengthens us for the work ahead.

A PRIESTHOOD
OF TRUTH

....

In George MacDonald's book *The Princess and Curdie*, Curdie is a changed man. A few years earlier, he did everything with a purpose. But now his faith is collapsing. He is beginning to lose a grasp on the mission. He is losing faith in the supernatural; he is forgetting that good exists; he begins to falter in his worldview. The purpose of the kingdom has become secondary to him.

One day while he is hunting, he shoots a white pigeon, and when he sees the pigeon's misery, a mysterious woman appears and confronts him concerning his doubts. Slowly, Curdie begins to see his disbelief and how quickly he lost a sense of the holy and supernatural. He confesses, and then suddenly, the pigeon is brought back to life. There is resurrection in confession. Curdie's hands are now clean, so the Old Princess sends him a mission, and he is told to keep his bow and arrow—to use his weapons for the good of society.

Our faith is not empty. We are full-bodied Christians sent on a mission by the Lord of glory, who commissioned us to go forth and make disciples of every nation, baptizing the nations into our story. While there are seasons of our lives when we may be uncertain about our mission, our task is to remind one another of who we are and what we are called to do.

This is what the priesthood of the believers means: that we are priests unto each other. It has become popular to think that the priesthood of all believers is a call to an isolated mission interpreting the Scriptures outside of a community. But the priesthood means that we join a sacred assembly, walking together armored and ready to fight the schemes of the Devil. We put on a new priesthood, because priests take their calling from the Lord who was called and never ceased to war for our salvation.

We should not doubt our mission, but persevere and put on the armor of God. We need to depend on God's wisdom, trusting the old wise sayings of Lady Wisdom to guide us as we march in God's armor.

The Apostle exhorts you to fight boldly for truth, righteousness, and the kingdom. There is no dark force or power that can overcome the armor of God when you trust in his might. As John Calvin concludes: "Nor will any who, with his assistance, fight against Satan, fail in the day of battle."[20]

----

20   John Calvin's commentary on *Ephesians* (Grand Rapids, MI: Baker Books), p. 337.

THE ORIGIN OF PAUL'S METAPHOR

The stage now is set for the mission. But we need to determine the source of Paul's metaphor.

We know that broadly, Paul is alluding to God's own armor which he wears in battle.

King Saul wanted to impose a manmade armory on David to fight Goliath, to dress David like a common warrior. But the battle belongs to the Lord, so God dressed David with Himself. Yahweh of Hosts is the saint's armor.

Similarly, Satan offered Jesus alternative armors in the wilderness, but Jesus knew that the battle belonged to Yahweh. Instead, he put on the righteousness of God and fought against the greater Goliath, Satan.

In the Garden, Satan tempted Adam to put on *his* armor, to doubt God's armor. Adam fell and was ashamed. But when the Christian puts on the armor of God, he is putting on Christ, the new Adam. Our Lord promises that he will never be ashamed. Every Christian is called to put on Christ, and Christ will lead him into battle. We do not rely on worldly wisdom, but conduct ourselves with godly sincerity (2 Corinthians 1:12).

Some have argued that Paul borrowed this metaphor from a Roman soldier. Paul would be addressing an audience familiar with the gladiatorial games at the stadium and amply familiar with the battle armor of a Roman soldier.[21] The Roman soldier was known for his brutality, strength, and discipline. Therefore, Paul's argument would be a fitting analogy, with the Roman centurion preparing himself to face the enemy.

While certain analogies may fit, it would be difficult to substantiate this claim since there is nothing intrinsically Christian about the Roman soldier. They served anti-Christian lords and rulers. We may even say that they submitted to the spiritual forces of evil in their day. They shared in the unholiness of the empire, while Paul is describing an armor rooted in Christian virtue—one which includes discipline and might not used for nefarious purposes, but for good works.

So what is the background to Paul's description?

THE PRIESTLY ARMOR

Peter tells us that God is forming a holy priesthood (1 Peter 2:5-9). Paul refers to his proclamation of the gospel as priestly duties (Romans 15:16), which serve to convert the Gentiles to Jesus Christ. Paul's vocabulary comes directly from the Old Testament. God inspires Paul to use this biblical vocabulary to communicate. As we will see, his armor is borrowed from the priestly garments.

....

21 Gerald F. Hawthorne, Ralph P. Martin, and Daniel G. Reid, eds., "Ephesians," *Dictionary of Paul and His Letters: A Compendium of Contemporary Biblical Scholarship* (Downers Grove, IL: InterVarsity Press, 1993), p. 250. See also John F. Shean, *Soldiering for God: Christianity and the Roman Army* (History of Warfare, vol. 61); and Pat Southern, *The Roman Army: A Social and Institutional History.*

Priests reflected God's holy ways to the nations.

The priestly theme goes all the way back to Adam, who was called to be a priest in the Garden. He was to be a protector of all things. He was to care for and lead his wife in proper worship, but he failed as a priest. His armor was not established in truth. The serpent deceived him.

Jesus came later as a faithful priest and repeatedly spoke the truth: "It is written … It is written … It is written …" Our Lord directs our attention to the truth found in God's revelation—that word above all earthly powers.

United to Jesus, we put on garments of truth and are robed in the power and might of Jesus. Faithful priests know that the devils of our culture will speak poorly of our armor, that they will mock the way we act, the way we speak, the truth we uphold, and every other virtue we cherish. But we proclaim the truth because Christ has given us his righteousness to wear.

THE BELT OF TRUTH

Paul begins his list by establishing the most important part of this armor, which begins with truth:

> **Stand therefore, having fastened on the belt of truth …** EPHESIANS 6:14a

In the ordination of Aaron and his sons, we receive a description of this belt:

> **And Moses brought Aaron and his sons
> and washed them with water. And he put
> the coat on him and tied the sash around
> his waist and clothed him with the robe
> and put the ephod on him and tied the
> skillfully woven band of the ephod
> around him, binding it to him with the
> band.** LEVITICUS 8:6-7

Part of a priest's outfit is the sash around his waist. When you read the description of the priestly garments, you know there is a lot of symbolism invested. The colors on the priest match the colors of the holy place.[22] This was important because the place of worship needed to reflect the holiness of the priest.

So, the priest's clothing symbolized the people's worship. What happens if you have an unclean priest? You have unclean worship. When priests came to the presence of God, the people knew that God stood before them.

The priests were fastened by truth, because truth was the only proclamation that would strengthen their word before God. God does not tolerate falsehood, which is why priests needed to be washed in truth before coming to the great truth-teller. If priests did not affirm truth, they

....

22　The belt, or "girdle," worn by the High Priest was of fine linen with "embroidered work" in blue, purple and scarlet (Exodus 28:39, 39:29).

were bound to lead the people astray, and the worship of God's people would be corrupted.[23]

Before we delve deeper into the definition of truth, it will be helpful to note what truth is *not*.

Truth is not an excellent liturgy, gorgeous cathedrals, or priestly rituals. How many gorgeous cathedrals exist today, especially in Europe, with remarkable choirs and a thousand-year-old architecture, where truth is nowhere to be found in the pulpit or in the life of the people? They are white-washed tombs masqueraded in outward glory. These monuments have the appearance of truth, but they rot in their falsehoods. Their priests may dress themselves with precious stones and even put on a sash, but they are the blind leading the blind.

Man looks on the outside, but God looks at the inner truth. He sees beyond the ostentatious displays to the heart of the matter.

James B. Jordan says, "Worship is not a way of getting into the sanctuary, it is a response to truth."[24] If a church has the best worship practices and all the distinctive practices you desire but does not abide in the truth, this is all in vain.

What we see on the screen of churches today is not the real display, but an edited version corrupting the fabric of truth. Outward architectural harmony is not

---

23 See Ezekiel 22:26: Priests "have done violence" to God's word, and therefore have desecrated holy things, and profaned God's sabbath.
24 James B. Jordan's lectures on Ephesians, wordmp3.com

truth unless it displays the true Christ and the reality his truth envisions for us as priests.

Some years ago, I officiated a wedding in a beautiful building with perfect acoustics and gorgeous architecture. I sought out a congregation member who had experienced some of its history. I began conversing with the organist, who had been there for 35 years. He proudly told me that even though the church was down to only 100 members, the best way forward, to restore the old glory, was to rid ourselves of the male/female distinctions. He argued that if the church broke that old-fashioned barrier, then the people would flock back.

But what is the worth of sitting around beauty while the truth is absent? Beauty alone without truth does not provide lasting change. History is replete with examples of such travesties. Churches grounded in truth are more than decorative pieces; they fix their eyes on Jesus and his revelation.

WHAT IS TRUTH?

What is Truth? What does it mean to have the belt of truth fastened?

Truth is a Person and His work.

The Christian fastens the belt of truth because Jesus is the way, the truth, and the life (John 14:6). Our priestly belt is a response to the reality of the God-Man who spoke the world into existence and who sanctifies us in truth, because his word is true (John 17:17).

The Apostle Paul believes that when the Church fastens on the belt of truth, then goodness, beauty, and other virtues flow from it. Truth is the security of the armor. It binds everything else together. We do not need Saul's big and loose armor; you want an armor that fits just right and is adjusted according to truth. The entire armor is fastened by truth, and therefore, the Christian is always fitted for it.

Hundreds of years before Paul, the prophet Jeremiah warned the people of Israel that the Lord would punish them. Why? "…Truth has perished; it is cut off from their lips" (Jeremiah 7:28b). When truth—articulating the words of God—is absent from the lips of the people, and when a culture is too comfortable around us, our priestly garments are unfastened like the end of a Thanksgiving meal.

We cannot do that when it comes to the armor of God. If we do so, we lose the ability to stand firm against the rulers and authorities. It is a sign that we are unequipped for warfare.

The reason so many in our culture do not want to enter the war against Satan's wicked schemes is that it is easier to sacrifice our convictions and principles at the altar of false gods. But our High-Priest, Jesus, calls us to bring his truth to every square inch of civilization by the power of the Spirit. Like Curdie, we wash our hands clean and stand firm for the mission ahead.

We will be held accountable for our deeds. We will be held accountable for the many times we were more comfortable being covered in fig leaves than putting on the armor of God. But we must stand firm, because there is work to do and truth to tell. While God provides us with the armor, we are responsible to put it on and fight in the strength of his might.

PRAYER, DOMINION, AND FAITHFULNESS

Here are three ways in which the truth can be the piece that holds the entire armor together.

First, increase the vocabulary of your prayers. If truth speaks a God-given reality into the world, then praying must be central to its practice. We begin practicing truth best by communicating with the God of truth. You need to diversify the language you use in your petitions. This includes the use of imprecation in prayers. We are sometimes afraid or timid to speak the truth to the world because we are afraid of speaking against the world. The Psalmist was not. "Break the teeth of the wicked, O Lord." (See Psalm 3.) "Declare them guilty, O Lord!" (See Psalm 5.) "Rise up and confront them, O Lord." (See Psalm 17.) Truth demands conforming your words to the prayers of the Bible.

Secondly, understand that your task is dominion. Your agenda is to repair the broken pieces and rearrange the furniture of God's creation. This dominion task may include giving yourself to learning in community, singing heartily on the Lord's Day, engaging one another in word and deed in a way that honors Christ, delving into the study of Scriptures, engaging your leaders in the Church and community, and more directly, finding where truth has been absent in your life. Your calling is to be an ambassador of truth: to see the world around you upside down, and to contribute to turning it to its rightful order and place.

Thirdly, be faithful to the little things. As you see people doing what some would consider gigantic things, do not think for a moment that your territory is insignificant. Your calling is to be faithful where you are. Truth is believing that the Person of Christ is who he says he is. You may doubt at times whether what you are doing has any meaning; you may doubt whether your identity is secure in him, or why you have not been gifted as the other person. But when you fasten the belt of truth, when you trust in the provision of King Jesus for you, you will learn that you are secure in whatever you do.

Many years ago, a young lady in our congregation was diagnosed with a debilitating disease. Her entire life was changed. Suddenly, her routine went from normal, to one doctor after another. Sometimes she would travel out of state to see specialists who tried to discern what she had. They tried everything and while there was some improvement, in the end, she was back to bedrest.

She suffered well, though I am sure she had moments of confusion, wondering why God added this suffering to her life. One day she was reflecting on her life and called me and said, "Pastor, I think I know how to think about life."

I said, "I am so glad to hear that."

She said, "My life belongs to Jesus, and if this is where Jesus has placed me, then my role will be to encourage others with his truth." So she did. She began to write notes and texts to people, and after a while, she understood what the Heidelberg Catechism says: *I am not my own, but belong, body and soul, to my Savior Jesus Christ.*[25]

Despite her weakness, she used her life to minister to so many. Truth is not a task for only the healthy; it is a task to all who participate in this vision of proclaiming God's reality to a world living by lies. Be faithful in your journey, and the God of all truth will keep you in Christ Jesus.

---

25 Heidelberg Catechism, Answer 1.

A MINISTRY OF
DISCERNMENT

....

I n C.S. Lewis' *Prince Caspian*, the Pevensie children
return to Narnia. When they do, they discover that
there are new rulers. The animals which were once
invested in Narnian life have now retreated. They do
not communicate any longer. They are under tyranny.
The new reality keeps the children from seeing things as
they are—except for Lucy, who sees Aslan and believes
he has returned. The others doubt the story. When Aslan
is finally revealed, there is a deep sense of shame among
them. Susan perhaps felt it most painfully, and Aslan saw
her and addressed her:

> *Susan, you have listened to fears, child.*
> *Come, let me breathe on you. Forget them*
> *and be brave again.*[26]

Paul says, "God gave us a spirit not of fear but
of power and love and self-control" (2 Timothy 1:7).
When reality changes in our lives, or even when truth

....

26   C.S. Lewis, *Prince Caspian* (Geoffrey Bles, 1951).

seems absent, our default reaction is fear. God often comes in our fears, dismay, and loss of wonder.

Sometimes we fail to see God working in our midst because we have accepted the arguments of this world. We have lost the ability to discern what is good and evil, and we miss the works of God right in front of us—and often we miss God himself.

When we think of the history of Israel, we can say that the Old Testament priesthood had lost the magic of Eden. They had forgotten the glory-cloud, the miracles, the covenant, the delicious vegetation, and the intimacy with God. When you leave Eden for a while, you lose the habits and forget the beauty of the place you once called home.

But on the day of Pentecost, God breathed his Spirit on us and gave us new courage to fight the conspirators who seek to destroy our land. Eden is our land, and we cannot allow the false priests to take over.

Sometimes our fears come through the news. But often, they come through our relationships. We build relationships around people who do not give us the courage to fasten the belt of truth. We may surround ourselves with people who constantly criticize our actions and make light of any progress we make. If we accomplish something, they say, "Well, that's not much." If we move towards a bold action, they will say, "That's not bold enough." These kinds of people do not provide incentives for godly living, nor do they encourage walking in step with the Spirit. It may be that you need new friends, new encouragers, and new psalm singers to walk alongside you.

The Apostle Paul did not feel the need to correct every little thing the Ephesians did. He reserved most of his writings to encourage. In his parallel passage in 1 Thessalonians 5, the Apostle does not go into great detail in illustrating the armor of God, but he does offer a clear picture:

> **But since we belong to the day, let us be sober, having put on the breastplate of faith and love, and for a helmet the hope of salvation.** 1 THESSALONIANS 5:8

He concludes:

> **Therefore encourage one another and build one another up, just as you are doing.** 1 THESSALONIANS 5:11

Paul uses the armor of God as a means to encourage the saints. *Encouragement* means "to speak fruitfully into the life of another." But how is this done when people are panicking about their stocks, or their children's poor decisions, or whether they will find a job, a good wife or husband, or whether we will all die in the next natural catastrophe? Anxiety can run from significant issues to all the little ones. We are prone to wander and lose our grip on truth.

It is quite clear that for Paul, encouragement strengthens our understanding of the future and our resolve to stand firm. The armor of God provides us with a good eschatology. We are confident that the future will work in our favor because, ultimately, God is our all in all—the God of hope. He clothes us for warfare and encourages our hearts.

Likewise, Paul's closing words in Ephesians function like a motivational speech, a masterpiece of encouragement. This is Paul's unrelenting push to the finish line. It's as if he is saying, "Carry on! Put this armor on when things get complicated. When things don't make sense, put on the armor anyway!"

He lays down some excellent ground rules for the Church and then takes a few verses to encourage the saints in their walk.

Paul was a man who understood suffering, who knew intimately what it meant to be falsely accused, who followed Jesus in a prison cell and in front of Roman leaders and false teachers. But he stood firm, having put on the armor of God throughout his life. He is telling the Christians, "The power of Jesus is sufficient to carry you to the end of the course."

The Apostle's basis for encouragement was the life, death and resurrection glory of Jesus, sealed in the vindication of his work when he ascended to the Father's right hand. Truth fastens the belt, but Paul offers another essential feature of this armor, which invites us further into this life of truth.

THE BREASTPLATE OF RIGHTEOUSNESS

> **Stand therefore, having fastened on the belt of truth, and having put on the breastplate of righteousness ...**
>
> EPHESIANS 6:14

We already mentioned that truth is what secures us. Truth is a Person and His work for us. Truth makes our armor efficient. If you take that away, we are vulnerable morally and theologically. How many of us have fallen because we have failed to tighten our belt with the truth?

Everything we do is a response to that reality. We do not put on the armor in search of truth; we put on truth. Paul says elsewhere, "But put on the Lord Jesus Christ, and make no provision for the flesh, to gratify its desires" (Romans 13:14).

Where do we go once truth is fastened? Next, we put on the breastplate of righteousness.

Again, contrary to popular opinion, Paul is not looking up at a Roman soldier from a prison cell, designing his attire for his final speech. Instead, he uses analogies from Old Testament with great ease, throughout his writings. The Old Testament is Paul's first language, and he uses his native tongue to communicate in all other languages. Paul is talking about the clothing we put on as priests unto God. He uses the analogy of the armor not to connect us with Roman soldiers, but to connect us with priestly warriors.

Our clothing reflects the priestly garments of the Old Testament just as it reflects the priestly garments of Jesus. Jesus is never compared to a Roman soldier, but is a great High-Priest who sympathizes with our weaknesses and calls us to hold firmly to the faith (Hebrews 4:14-16).

When we connect these references, we can see why this priestly element was necessary for Paul's description. The Apostle is continuing in the same war story of Aaron, Isaiah, and Jesus. He follows in their train. As priests unto God, we follow the priests and prophets in pursuing righteousness.

Righteousness exalts a nation, but sin condemns the people (Proverbs 14:34). Sin keeps priests from making good judgments and discerning the needs of the people. The breastplate of righteousness delivers the people from bearing false witness and trains God's priests to discern his will for their lives.

Adam failed to deliver Eve from the schemes of Satan because he did not discern God's Word. Mankind fell into sin and misery because the first priest did not put on the breastplate of righteousness. He failed to pass judgment on the Serpent. His heart was exposed to false words, and he could not understand truth from error.

But Christ overcame the temptations of the Devil in the wilderness, and he passed judgment on the religious leaders of the day. He upheld righteousness for the nations. He became the Urim and Thummim for the people when he embodied righteousness in his own ministry.

The breastplate is the part that protects vital organs, especially the heart. It is the part of the armor that encourages discernment, and protects you from ethical misgivings. The breastplate of righteousness gives you the wisdom to see Aslan and not doubt him, to make necessary judgments in friendships, personal decisions, and various life choices.

Paul encourages us to renew our covenant with God and man, to seek redemption from those habits that entangle us in sin. We will find refuge in the righteous God when the breastplate is secure. We put on the breastplate of righteousness to indicate to the enemy that we can discern falsehoods and proclaim the judgment of God through prayers of blessings and imprecations. We should never forsake righteousness in our dealings as priests. God encourages and equips us to fight with discernment.

In 2 Chronicles 18, Jehoshaphat deals with the king of Israel, Ahab. They were going to war together, but Ahab told Jehoshaphat, "You wear my robes in war, and I will go in disguise." The enemy eventually figured out that Jehoshaphat was not the king of Israel, and then the text says:

> **But a certain man drew his bow at random and struck the king of Israel between the scale armor and the breastplate. Therefore he said to the driver of his chariot, "Turn around and carry me out of the battle, for I am wounded"...Then at sunset he died.**
>
> 2 CHRONICLES 18:33-34

When righteousness is forsaken, the heart is exposed, and death is near.

Did you hear the description? A "bow at random..." Some refer to this as comedic relief, or perhaps a divine way of mocking evil man's attempts to take off God's armor and act by their own strength. Both interpretations are a fitting description of man's attempts to go to war with alternative armors.

There is no luck or randomness in warfare. In God's war story, that arrow hit precisely where it was meant. When righteousness is absent, you cannot hide from God's "random" arrows.

MOVING FROM
GLORY TO GLORY

....

C hristians move with the belt of truth and the
breastplate of righteousness. Truth is essentially
first, like light was essentially first in creation. We might
say the truth is the worldview through which we read
the other pieces of the armor.

Then, the Apostle moves to the revelation of God.
The breastplate of righteousness is the will of God for
the nations. We uphold that when we sing, pray, and
proclaim God's justice. We are saying that the righteous
Judge will do all things well.

Remember that the Apostle urges the Ephesian
Christians to "stand" three times in this chapter. Paul
alludes to many texts in the Old Testament where God's
people are summoned to stand firm. In Exodus 14 and
2 Chronicles 1, God's leaders command the people to
stand firm as they prepare to fight their enemies.

God's people stand firm because they know that there
is One who has gone before us and delivered us from evil.

We know that if we stand firm to the end, we will see the salvation of Yahweh.

THE SHOES OF READINESS

That language is the background for much of what Paul describes in the following piece of the priestly armor:

> **...And, as shoes for your feet, having put on the readiness given by the gospel of peace.** EPHESIANS 6:15

Priests represent God to the people and instruct them in what God expects of them (Leviticus 10:10-11). As the priests went, so did the people. It was imperative to have faithful priests who lived sacrificially and offered pure sacrifice.

But in the New Covenant, we are all priests unto God. We walk boldly into the holy of holies because now we, too, have access to the sanctuary of God. We no longer need priests to go in our stead because Christ has torn the veil from top to bottom, transforming the old sacrificial hierarchy. Now, we enter into the throne of grace as servants of the Great High-Priest who went before us. We are his priests entering into the Heavenly places.

Our bodies are living sacrifices to God as spiritual worship (Romans 12:1-12). We still need representatives—pastors—to proclaim and administer the sacraments, but Paul is not talking about that kind of specific ministry; he refers to the broad priesthood of the Church.

As priests, we wear the armor of God as evangelists to the nations. We must be hospitable evangelists, friendly evangelists, liturgical evangelists, and singing evangelists. This evangelistic theme is at the heart of Paul's reference to the "shoes for your feet."

PRIESTLY FEET

When Moses comes before the burning bush in Exodus, he is told to remove his sandals, for the place he stands is holy (Exodus 3:5). Priests are barefooted when they come into God's presence. Even in Roman Catholic Missals today, priests remove their shoes before venerating the cross on Good Friday.[27] This uncovering of the feet was necessary for the temple courts and holy places where God's presence dwelt.

But when God's people ate at the Passover, they needed sandals on their feet.

> **In this manner you shall eat it: with your belt fastened, your sandals on your feet, and your staff in your hand. And**

---

27 I believe Nestorian priests processed into the Church barefoot. In the Armenian Apostolic Churches, the priests remove their shoes when approaching the altar (or so I have been told).

you shall eat it in haste. It is the LORD's Passover. EXODUS 12:11

The feasts were corporate activities in the life of the Church. This aligns quite well with Paul's exhortation.

The armor entailed a preparedness for warfare. David picks up this theme in Psalm 23, where he says that Yahweh prepares a table for us in the presence of our enemies. God's people are ready for war, even when they eat. Their feet are covered because they are in the posture of warfare.

The prophet Isaiah also continues this theme when speaking of the evangelistic task of the saints:

How beautiful upon the mountains are the feet of him who brings good news, who publishes peace, who brings good news of happiness, who publishes salvation, who says to Zion, "Your God reigns." ISAIAH 52:7

The priest came to bring glad tidings of peace and salvation. According to the prophet, their feet are associated with blessings to the people.

The feet are related to how you find righteousness or unrighteousness in the Old Testament. Proverbs 9:6 says, "Leave your simple ways and you will live; walk in the way of insight." Some feet walk toward holiness, and others towards misery. But the Scriptures praise those whose feet bring light rather than darkness.

The Apostle Paul has an abundant resource of images to work with as he urges the saints to treasure something about our feet. It is rather interesting how the Bible speaks positively of the feet. It is the part of the body that is most washed in the Bible, because it carries a tremendous responsibility to carry messages around. You need to protect your feet to protect your ability to communicate the truth.

> **And how are they to preach unless they are sent? As it is written, "How beautiful are the feet of those who preach the good news!"** ROMANS 10:15

Finally, in Jesus' ministry, he gives the disciples specific actions to take with their feet:

> **And if anyone will not receive you or listen to your words, shake off the dust from your feet when you leave that house or town.** MATTHEW 10:14

The feet indicate blessings to those who hear and judgment to those who reject the claims of our Lord. This theme goes back to the first promise in Genesis 3:15. The promise that the seed of the woman would crush the head of the serpent is fulfilled when Jesus crushes the head of Satan with his feet (Romans 16:20). Satan's schemes of lies and kingdom opposition led to his demise when Jesus brought peace to all those who trust in him.

Our Lord even established a ritual of feet washing (John 13), which served to prepare his disciples to ready themselves for the task of spreading the kingdom, even if it meant they would die for it. Foot washing commemorated God's cleansing of his priesthood to go and disciple the nations (Matthew 28:18-20).

THE READY POSTURE

The Apostle urges a "readiness" posture when putting the shoes on our feet. Shoes are for marching and moving. The implication is that you are moving towards something or someone, to bring something to someone. The armor compels us to move forward in our mission as priests.

These movements will sometimes cause pain as the gospel of peace may lead to divisions among family and friends (Matthew 10:34-39). But Jesus attaches a promise to those who walk worthy of their armor: some may lose their lives, but in so doing, they will find life in him.

While Old Testament priests walked barefooted because of the holiness laws, Paul built this armor on the new reality of Jesus' life, death, resurrection, and ascension. We do not need to walk barefooted anymore. Christ has become our shoes, and our readiness.

When Jesus died, the veil was torn from top to bottom, and the wall of partition was broken down. Heaven has come down to meet us in the person of

Jesus Christ. Now, the holy priesthood walks with shoes because we walk with the King of Kings who has made us holy unto God and dwells with us by the power of the Spirit. We are indwelt temples. All spaces are made holy through Jesus Christ. The royal priesthood walks throughout the world, because we are heirs of the world (Romans 4:13).

Still, our temptation will be to walk barefooted through life. We don't want gravel. No hard terrain; just smooth, white sand. But Paul places us in constant preparedness. We will have to walk through hard places—but remember that God has prepared us with his shoes. To have the shoes on our feet is to keep moving forward to proclaim the good news of peace and salvation.

Most of us live relatively uneventful lives. I do not believe for a moment that Paul desired us to engage in every fight that is before us. We are told to be wise in how and with whom we engage. "Answer not a fool according to his folly" (Proverbs 26:4a). So, we must be discerning.

But I also know that the Apostle Paul did not mean for our lives to be unchallenged. Sometimes we must "answer a fool according to his folly" (Proverbs 26:5a).

How, then, can we ready ourselves with shoes on our feet? How can we put on our shoes today differently than we did yesterday?

We must ask why our shoes seem so unused, when opportunities abound to proclaim the gospel of peace. If our understanding of this command leads us to walk around town passively, we have misunderstood Paul's description. The shoes on our feet are a call to a ready posture: Paul assumes that we are prepared to walk and move. And this entire march is predicated on the gospel of peace.

What John Calvin wrote in the 16th century is still very true in the 21st:

> *A rough road and many other obstacles slow our progress, and we are discouraged by the smallest annoyance.*[28]

How easily we take a break from our battles against evil! The smallest annoyance, and suddenly we throw our hands in despair. "Go ahead, rob me, Satan! Take away my belongings … I surrender."

But as one author said, we walk in "a long obedience in the same direction."[29] The gospel of peace does not make us settle down in our status. It makes us pursue a kingdom that shall have no end. It encourages us to walk towards bringing peace wherever the curse is found. The gospel gives us peace with God, and now we proclaim peace to others.

The shoes in this armor push us towards a fuller, public gospel rather than a comfortable, private religion.

---

28   John Calvin's commentary on *Ephesians* (Grand Rapids, MI: Baker Books).
29   This is the title of Eugene Peterson's book, *A Long Obedience in the Same Direction: Discipleship in an Instant Society* (InterVarsity Press, 2021).

In C.S. Lewis' fictional work, the experienced demon, Screwtape, urges his apprentice, Wormwood, to tempt Christians with a noncommittal religion. He notes … "A moderated religion is as good for us as no religion at all—and more amusing."[30] How amusing we must be to the Devil when we choose the bare minimum: to show up on Sundays and walk poorly through the week. We act as if we retired our shoes, and are now on a perpetual vacation from the armor of God. We know that Satan has a long-term strategy, which is why he has an advantage over so many of us who think only in the *now*.

To what is our life leading? A few minutes of niceties at a funeral, or an actual inheritance to our children and communities? Too many live lives as if they are content with a few nice words at death, but those who put on the armor of God live in order to leave an inheritance of truth, faithfulness, peace, godliness, steadfastness, consistency, fruitfulness, and repentance.

God has made us be on the offensive against evil, not to be an amusement park for devils. When the Apostle Paul gives us these imperatives, he is not looking for fault or putting on a critical spirit or even operating in a better-than-thou category; he is giving us a motivational speech to press on toward the goal for the prize of the upward call of God in Christ Jesus (Ephesians 3:14). He wants your pursuit of righteousness and peace to

....

30   C.S. Lewis, *The Screwtape Letters* (Geoffrey Bles, 1942).

be reasons for the kingdom to rejoice. Take it to heart. Put the shoes on your feet and be ready to proclaim the Gospel of peace.

A TOTALISTIC
FAITH

....

L et's do a little review.
First, the belt of truth is the security of the armor. Truth is a Person and his Work for us. Without truth, our armor will not endure. When we put on the armor of God, we are putting on Christ.

Second, the breastplate of righteousness is what we put on to make good decisions and to judge rightly. It is the discerning ministry of the Christian. Righteousness in the Bible pertains to renewal and redemption. God's righteousness for the nations is his judgment to vindicate the righteous and destroy the wicked schemes of evil men. Righteousness restores the world by undoing the effects of the Fall and transforming our dispositions.

Third, the shoes of the armor speak to our willingness to move forward in uncomfortable situations. When you find yourself next to someone longing for peace or hope, they ultimately long for Jesus. If your shoes are on, you will take the opportunities in front of you and bear witness to the peace of the gospel by speaking life into them when all they have is death and misery.

The shoes of the armor can feel quite intimidating when we are not willing to season the lives of others with salt (Colossians 4:6). The shoes on our feet may ensure a life of incivility from others, or it may secure a life of persecution, as it did with our forefathers—or even death, as the martyrs testify. But ordinarily, it will put you at odds with the things of this world. It will give you a worldview often despised in our present culture. Our duty, then, is to keep walking faithfully.

When I was a child, one of the missionaries we supported came to town to visit our congregation. He came into town during the week and decided to walk around the city. As he walked to a local shop, a vehicle approached him. The men inside the car opened the door and demanded his wallet.

The missionary said, "I will give it to you, but you have to take me with you in the car." The men were puzzled, but heeded his strange request. The missionary spent over an hour telling these men about the love of Jesus, how God views stealing as sinful, and that he demands restitution for their sins. The men were so moved by his witness that they dropped him off at the same store, voluntarily went to the police, and confessed to several other crimes.

As you can imagine, it made the news the next day. One of the men in our church pointedly asked the missionary, "What were you thinking?"

He said honestly, "I don't know, but I was ready!"

I would strongly discourage such a drastic move, but I would encourage all of us to assume such a ready posture. Remember: you can leave an inheritance, or you can live for a few nice words in a eulogy. It is impossible to treat the faith with seriousness and soberness if you do not commit to wearing the priestly armor of God.

ACTIVATING THE ARMOR

The Church is plagued by spiritual apathy and laziness. The Apostle Paul calls us to sit up straight and put on the armor of God with boldness. He now builds on this armory with a fourth piece, which activates the whole armor of God.

> **In all circumstances take up the shield of faith, with which you can extinguish all the flaming darts of the evil one...**
>
> EPHESIANS 6:16

Satan wants to rob us of our confidence in Jesus and take away that which we most treasure. He wishes to diminish our faith by spiritualizing our worldview. If he succeeds in keeping our faith private and reserved only for spiritual acts of piety, the armor can remain ineffective.

But Paul has a different message altogether. The virtue that activates the armor of God in the world is faith—a faith so comprehensive that it cannot but take every thought captive to the obedience of Jesus Christ (2 Corinthians 10:5). The Apostle commands us to take up the shield of faith in all circumstances, because faith is how we mature in our walk. It naturally follows righteousness and the shoes of readiness, as Paul asserts in Romans:

> **For in it the righteousness of God is revealed from faith for faith, as it is written, "The righteous shall live by faith."** ROMANS 1:17

Yahweh comforted Abraham in a vision by saying:

> **Fear not, Abram, I am your shield; your reward shall be very great.** GENESIS 15:1

God is the Christian's shield, and the reward of those who trust in him will be great. The shield speaks of God's protection in virtually every case in the Psalms. "But you, O LORD, are a shield about me" (Psalm 3:3a). "... In whom I take refuge, my shield" (Psalm 18:2b). "Our soul waits for the LORD; he is our help and our shield" (Psalm 33:20).

Faith is the way the saints are protected from evil, or from a life of faithlessness and doubt. Faith is so crucial to the Christian armor that the Book of Hebrews reserves an entire chapter to honor the faith of the Old Testament priesthood, from Abel to the martyrs (Hebrews 11:1-40). They are said to live by faith even to the point of death (Hebrews 11:13). Their obedience was a faithful one because their faith was a living one. There is only one kind of faith—an obedient faith.

Jerry Bridges notes in his classic work, *The Pursuit of Holiness*:

> *Faith is not only necessary for salvation, it is also necessary to live pleasing to God. Faith enables us to claim the promises of God— but it also enables us to obey the commands of God. Faith enables us to obey when obedience is costly or seems unreasonable to the natural mind.*[31]

The shield of faith provides conviction and confidence in God's promises, which are yes and amen. The Scriptures urge Christians to believe in the promises of God, for, "Faith is the assurance of things hoped for, the conviction of things not seen" (Hebrews 11:1).

In the Old Testament, God gave commands which were difficult to believe, but God's people lived by faith. The people had to put on the shield of faith to obey God's word and wait to see the salvation of the Lord. Faith

....

31   Jerry Bridges, *The Pursuit of Holiness* (Minneapolis, MN: NavPress, 2006), p. 140.

activates the armor of God as we cast our cares on God, for he cares for us (1 Peter 5:7).

God's shield is all-encompassing, covering our entire body. We trust by faith that God protects us when we walk toward righteousness. The Roman soldier walked by sight, trusting in manmade weapons to keep them from harm. But the Christian priest walks by faith, because he believes our God defends and guards us against the flaming darts of the unfaithful and unclean.

The shield does not refer to a piece of the priestly garment, but to the priest's trust in God to fulfill what he said he would. When sacrifices were offered, the priest could trust in God's promise of forgiveness. When the priest came before God, he could trust that God would keep the worship pure.

THE TOTALITY OF FAITH

The shield of faith is the priest's trust in God's covenant, that God will keep his promises to Israel's priesthood. The shield of faith is the certainty that God's promises will surround the people of God as long as faith guides their system of covenant renewal—as long as it does not compromise the purity of worship. Again, the shield of faith is the priest's trust that God will keep him safe from corruption.

That is why the command to "take up" is preceded by the exhaustive claim to do so "in all circumstances." Paul gives you no way out. He does not say, "When you get up in a good mood," "When you get a better job," or "When it's a beautiful, sunny day." Even when things don't make sense, we take up the shield of faith, because faith is exercised in the midst of the known and unknown.

Israel was to be a light to the nations. The shield of faith is the armor piece that gives us the confidence to serve Jesus and activate the armor in the ordinary. Even the word *confidence* carries this sense in its etymology. To be confident is to go forth with (*con*) faith (*fide*).

The shield of faith is the gospel confidence to not grow weary in well-doing, to not allow the temptation to draw you like a pied piper. Instead, it is the confidence to see a difficult situation and move according to God's promises.

But these seem like abstract ideas. How do we get there? What does faith do to make me so bold in the face of challenges?

Abel offered a better sacrifice, Noah built an ark, and Abraham obeyed when everything called him to let go of faith. Yet the call to leave an inheritance was greater than a few words in an eulogy. The shield of faith moves forward knowing that God does all things well, surprises us daily with his mercies, and knows the end of the story even when we don't have a clue. The shield of faith knows that if the heart is clean, the enemy's flaming darts will pose no threat.

You may have seen movies where an imposing army is coming at you, but your leader says, "Hold!" Then, you hold! The opposing soldiers get closer. Your leader says, "Shield." When you put up your shield, you are not getting ready to die, but readying to attack. Faith sees the difficulties and prepares for them so it can attack the enemy accordingly.

Let's assume you have this impossible task ahead of you: a difficult conversation, a complicated event, a conflict with an unbelieving friend, relative or co-worker, increasing debt, a challenging marriage, or whatever it may be. How do you put on the shield of faith as a gospel man or woman? That is the real question.

Activated faith relies on three principles:[32]

1. NORMATIVE. The Word of God speaks directly to all circumstances. The Bible may not say, "Thou shalt get this job and not that job," but it does say how to make a wise decision concerning a calling. It will teach you how to pursue wisdom so that you know what corrupts your calling as a priest unto God.

2. SITUATIONAL. Every situation requires godly counselors around you. Generally, you do not consult people who love you, because pride compels you to look to no one but yourself. But one who puts on the shield of faith will surround himself with faithful pastors, teachers, parents, and counselors who love him and have his well-being in mind. The shield of faith demands investment in the community of wisdom wherever God places you.

....

32 These principles are adjustments to John Frame's tri-perspectival model of theology.

3. EXISTENTIAL. This speaks to our emotions. Martin Luther talked about this quite a bit, and as someone frequently attacked for his faith, he is someone to heed. Luther was deeply troubled by the Devil's attacks, but he knew when to put on the shield of faith against our great enemy:

> So when the Devil throws your sins in your face and declares that you deserve death and hell, tell him this: "I admit that I deserve death and hell, what of it? For I know One who suffered and made satisfaction on my behalf. His name is Jesus Christ, Son of God, and where He is there I shall be also!"[33]

Luther understood that his conscience and emotions were bound by his loyalty to Jesus—the belt of truth. Our God-given conscience tells us daily whether we live by faith or by sight. When we do something against God's revelation, the Holy Spirit convicts us of sin (John 16:8). The shield of faith shapes our conscience and emotions.

Paul was quite bold when he said to put on the shield of faith in all circumstances. The result is that it will extinguish all the flaming darts of the evil one. The Apostle assumed an ongoing war for your body and soul. He was not being naïve; he understood that we would

....

33   Martin Luther, *Letters of Spiritual Counsel*, translated and edited by Theodore G. Tappert (Vancouver, British Columbia: Regent College, 2003), pp. 86–87.

fall short of the glory of God. But Paul believed that faith is part of a larger strategy, a pattern of life.

Christians are not defined by a few poor decisions here and there. We are image-bearers whose lives are shaped by thousands of small and big decisions. To put on the shield of faith is to set the course for the long journey.

Our Lord Jesus looked to the cross as the culmination of that journey. He was baptized, warred well against evil, and proclaimed liberty to the captives. Jesus trusted in the Word of God as he journeyed in union with the Father and the Spirit, and a deep and abiding faith shaped his human conscience. The saint follows that journey of faith with the full knowledge that Christ has gone before us.

A BAPTISMAL
ATTIRE

....

When we consider the armor of God, we tend to picture an armor that is perhaps too complicated to put on daily. We guard against impurity as priests, but as Paul affirms, it is far more bearable and fruitful to put this armor on if we understand that its role is to equip us to see the enemy and war against him. If we do not understand the extent of the devil's schemes, we will lose the motivation to put on Christ.

The Apostle calls us to stand firm; not to put up a fight or to give it our best shot. No, there is an actual enemy who will be happily satisfied if we stay away from this armor, or take it up leisurely.

This armor ought to be as common as breathing. The Christian duty is to armor up *each day*.

One of the premises of this book is that Paul is describing a priestly outfit, not the garments of a Roman soldier. After all, we are, as Peter says, a royal priesthood. The priesthood of the Old Testament draws its imagery from the priestly duties of the men called to serve in the holy places of Israel. The new priesthood, established in Jesus Christ, draws its images from the vast array of metaphors and physical descriptions of the priestly garment.

Exodus 28 presents one of the fuller pictures in the Torah concerning the priestly pattern. Its central purpose is to describe those who have access to the Lord's presence. When God communicates details of his portable residence in the Israelite encampment, the priests' clothing takes central stage because priests will be the sacred managers in this new building project. The materials used for their clothing match the material used for the construction of the tent.[34] There is a harmony between the priest's garments and the holy place. *Priest* and *place* function in an orderly fashion to describe the priest's role: to carry the people to the holy, and to bring the holy back to the people.

In the New Covenant, the priestly armor takes on new meaning, because Christ is our armor and our temple (John 2:21). Priests put on the righteousness of the Priest, who is our sacred place. Jesus is our priest, clothing, and holiness: "For in him all the fullness of God was pleased to dwell" (Colossians 1:19).

When we approach Paul's additional armor pieces, we need to remember that the priesthood is Christ-centric. Christ is our fortress because he put on the

....

34   T. Desmond Alexander, *Exodus* (Grand Rapids, MI: Baker Books, 2016), p. 159.

armor of God for our sake. Our Lord fought valiantly and secured salvation for all his people. Therefore, the armor is a response of gratitude to the God of our salvation.

THE PRIESTLY FOREHEAD

Paul moves now to the highest place of the human body: he encourages us to "take the helmet of salvation" (Ephesians 6:17a). The language Paul uses assumes that God has already provided this salvation for his priests and that we are called to assume this helmet as a sign and seal of our faith.

What do you think about when something is put on your head? If you have watched a royal coronation, you associate heads with ordination. Someone is entering a new status—a new king or a new priest. This is what Paul has in mind with the helmet of salvation. He is talking about an ordination service.

The description of Aaron's garments appears in Exodus 28. The portion that is salient for our consideration of the helmet comes at the end of the chapter, which reads:

> You shall make a plate of pure gold and engrave on it, like the engraving of a signet, 'Holy to the LORD.' And you shall fasten it on the turban by a cord of blue. It shall be on the front of the turban. It shall be on Aaron's forehead, and Aaron

shall bear any guilt from the holy things that the people of Israel consecrate as their holy gifts. It shall regularly be on his forehead, that they may be accepted before the LORD. EXODUS 28:36-38

The language on the gold plate attached to the turban confirms that Aaron is God's holy servant. He is consecrated to the Lord and has access to the holy place.[35] This holiness marker is on Aaron's head.

The Bible has a developed theology of the head, which appears as early as the revelation of the curse in Genesis 3, where a promise is given that the head of the seed of the Serpent shall be crushed. The head becomes the central piece of any body, whether human or institutional. Creation begins with structural distinctions, where the sun and the moon represent powers. They are heads of days and nights. Heads represent the centrality of power.

This is especially true regarding the rituals of Israel and their consecration to holiness. Priests were set apart to represent the people, and what they wore on their heads was significant to their identity. They assumed authority in the ceremonies of Israel and offered ascension offerings to God. This headship is not one that rules by force, but willingly serves those under its care.

....

35   T. Desmond Alexander, *Exodus* (Grand Rapids, MI: Baker Books, 2016), p. 160.

We can see examples of how the head becomes a crucial element of Israel's religion. It appears in the taking of Nazarite vows (Numbers 6), the binding of the words of God on the forehead of our children (Deuteronomy 6), the death of kings (Judges 9:53), the ordination of kings (1 Samuel 10:1), the destruction of false gods (1 Samuel 5:4), and the crucifixion of the Son of Man (Matthew 27:29).

When I was ordained to the gospel ministry, I knelt. There were ordained men all around me laying hands on me. But what I remember most are the hands of Reverend Mickey Schneider pressing down on my head. I felt the weight of it throughout the prayers spoken. What was communicated through the act of laying on hands was that the task ahead would be heavy. The ordination to the ministry is filled with weightiness. We must feel it on our heads.[36]

Ordination to the ministry was similar in the Old Testament. The priest took on a turban. He wore it to serve in the temple. The turban was a very detailed headpiece that looked like a helmet. Symbolic pieces were attached—like a blue cord on the front of the turban.[37]

In Exodus 28, we see that Aaron's forehead bore the mark of holiness. He was a representative of the people as he performed his priestly duties. Furthermore, the

36 Glory is heaviness (*kavod*). Ordination is the reception of glory unto more glory.
37 If you are fascinated by the use of colors in the Bible, the Hebrew word for "blue" is *tekelet*. It is the same word translated as "purple" or "violet." In other words, blue is a royal reference. It is the color of Lent and Advent in the Church calendar.

ceremony that followed the ordination of priests also placed the head at the forefront of the symbolic hierarchy. Exodus 29 develops this theme:

And you shall set the turban on his head and put the holy crown on the turban. You shall take the anointing oil and pour it on his head and anoint him....And the priesthood shall be theirs by a statute forever. Thus you shall ordain Aaron and his sons. — Exodus 29:7-9

Even before the anointing rite, Aaron and his sons were washed with water. The candidates for the priesthood were baptized, as a sign of cleansing and purity. While these details have a chronology, they are one ordination ceremony. The pouring of oil on the head of the priest was an ordination ritual that carried significance throughout the rest of the Scriptures—especially the baptismal theology in the New Testament.

BAPTISM IMAGERY

Baptism is the incorporation of something or someone into the realm of the holy.

In the Old Covenant, priests sprinkled blood everywhere. In 2 Kings it is referred to as a sprinkling of blood for a peace offering (2 Kings 16:13). Blood was sprinkled on animals and garments to set them apart for holy use. In Exodus 29, oil was poured on men's heads to consecrate them to service.

Later in the New Testament, the language of sprinkling and pouring was adopted by the Apostle

Paul for the same reasons: to make ordinary things holy. Paul uses the same vocabulary of himself that the Old Testament used for animals, furniture, and priests. The Apostle says that his life is being poured out as a drink offering (Philippians 2:17). Later, he says that the life of the Christian is a living sacrifice unto God, which is his spiritual worship (Romans 12:1-2). The Christian is a priestly anointed sacrifice unto God (Leviticus 1:4).

The theme of priestly anointing is tied to the theology of baptism in the New Testament. This connection becomes even more pertinent, because the Bible connects the Christian to the priest. We do not participate in ceremonial sacrifices as the priests of old did. However, we carry similar functions into the world, and our ceremonies still take on the same pattern as the priests of the Old Testament.

But if we are called a royal priesthood, the question is, "When do we become priests?"

The argument is one of connectionalism. There is a direct correlation between the ordination into priesthood in the Old Testament, and the ordination of God's people in the New Testament.

The Apostle Paul unequivocally states that as many as are baptized into Christ have put on Christ (Galatians 3:28). The armor that communicates salvation is Christ himself, and the way to put on Christ is to be baptized into him. We are ordained as priests to this new realm when we are baptized. When God anoints us, we take on the helmet of salvation.

The symbol for baptism in the Old Testament is the anointing with oil. In James 5:14, we read that when someone is sick and calls the elders, we are to anoint their heads. We are affirming the priesthood of that baptized Christian, symbolized by their head. The waters of blessings in the history of God's people come from above, not below. They fall from Heaven on our heads to establish us with the helmet of salvation.

In baptism, we take on a royal office as sons and daughters of the kingdom. The helmet of salvation is not the putting on of intellectual expertise or the academic work of scholars. The helmet of salvation is given to all who are baptized into Christ. It is not reserved for the elite, but to all whom the Lord our God calls. The helmet is the priestly turban on the forehead to indicate the saint's set-apartness for serving God and his people.

The helmet of salvation works together with truth, righteousness, evangelical zeal for the gospel of peace, and faith. The saint's baptism is meant to produce a living faith. Therefore, a baptism that neglects the whole armor is an empty baptism which, in due time, shall bring judgment.

FALSE ASSUMPTIONS OF
THE HOLY PRIESTHOOD

The armor of God is not reserved for only those who have achieved a certain intellectual status within their ranks, or affirm certain propositions. That is an unhelpful barrier to the priesthood—because there are children and adults who will never be able to articulate the faith or evangelize the lost, because they are not able to, physically or mentally. Does the kingdom of God suddenly close the doors to the least of these?

Not at all. Instead, the kingdom is open to all those who come to the fount of grace in baptism. The kingdom of priests is for the least of these, "for to such belongs the kingdom of heaven" (Matthew 19:14b).

Another false assumption is that the armor of God is only fitting for those with a priestly calling. That is, unless you are called to the mission field or to the church, you cannot be as holy or as noble in the eyes of God.

Our Lord Jesus calls us into every sphere of society to serve him—whether as police officers, architects, teachers, engineers, or whatever profession. The armor of God is for all priests, because we have all become priests unto God. Every field is a calling, because God gifted you for that field.

There is no hierarchy of calling in the kingdom; there are priestly callings to every place in the kingdom. The armor belongs to all those baptized into the Triune Name. When the Apostle speaks of the helmet of salvation, he calls us to embrace our royal ordination into the work of the Lord—wherever that is found.

The helmet of salvation is the Christian's baptism, which he is called to take with him wherever he goes. The helmet of salvation is the priestly turban that we put on to be ordained for the work of the Church, redeeming the world in every sphere, for that is how we carry the Name of God to the nations.

When we take on the helmet of salvation, we remember that God has given us a new identity. If you were baptized later in life, that meant an obvious change of allegiance. If you were baptized an infant, you have no memory of it, except in pictures or video. But children grow into their baptismal life because they are constantly confronted with a status which they have no choice but to receive by grace, through faith. And so, we ask,

"Who are you?" *I am a child of God.*

"What does it mean to be a child of God?" *It means that I belong to him, and he loves me.*[38]

In our evangelical culture, we are trained to expect the ways of God to be extraordinary: "Give me a show! Let me see an altar call with tears."

But in the Bible, the ways of God are far more ordinary, like water poured on a baby's head, like water on the head of a former Mormon or a new believer. God's ways and means come gently on our heads, like oil rolling

38 Rich Lusk, *I Belong to God: A Covenantal Catechism* (Monroe, LA: Athanasius Press, 2014).

down the head to the beard of the priests and prophets and kings. God's ways do not require the extraordinary.

We need to remind ourselves of the ordinary ways in which God comes near to us. He comes through baptism, which calls us to a life of service in the kingdom. In this kingdom, we often remember how God took water and poured it over us so that we might live a life of repentance.

Remember your baptism today—which is to say, "Take up the helmet of salvation."

CHANGING AND
BEING CHANGED

....

The sixth and final piece of the armor is the one Paul defines with precision:

> **... And the sword of the Spirit, which is the word of God.** EPHESIANS 6:17b

Sometimes the Word of God pushes us to study, consider, delve deeper, follow the rationale, and see how an idea comes into being. The previous five armor pieces required a little digging into the theology of priestly ordination.

But this final piece leaves no doubt. We don't need to wonder what the sword of the Spirit is, because Paul already tells us. The Apostle combines these ideas in Hebrews also when he says the Word of God is like a two-edged sword, piercing the human soul and Spirit (Hebrews 4:12). The Apostle John, too, records that the words coming from the mouth of Jesus are like a sharp, two-edged sword (Revelation 1:16).

When Adam and Eve were expelled from the Garden, God placed cherubim and a flaming sword to guard the way to the tree of life (Genesis 3:24). From the beginning, swords have had a protective role: swords defend against the invasion of the sacred.

Anyone attempting to take the sacred from us must be met with the Sword of the Spirit. Jesus does this in the wilderness when he tells the Devil three times, "It is written …" He does not say, "Let me consult the laws of the Greeks or Romans."

The helmet of salvation refers to baptism, so Paul now concludes with the Word. Word and sacrament cannot work without each other. You cannot have only the Word of God apart from baptism, bread, and wine. And what brings all these together is the Spirit of God.

The sword is not a random tool in the priestly arsenal; it is a distinctly Spirit-led element of priestly protection. Certainly, all of the other pieces of armor bear the presence of the Spirit. Still, the sword takes on a unique role because Peter attributes the very inspiration of God's words to the Spirit.

> **… but men spoke from God as they were carried along by the Holy Spirit.**
> 2 PETER 1:21b

The Spirit is the One who makes the entire armor of God move forward. The Spirit indwells men to speak the Word of God. We stand firm because we walk in step with the Spirit (Galatians 5:25), who leads us by the Word of God. The Spirit makes baptism effective, and the Bible living and active. The Spirit takes these means and changes us through them.

Priestly warriors do not walk according to the wisdom of this age, but the wisdom of God. The sword is a tool of death throughout the Old Testament.[39] Isaiah prophesies the coming Messianic figure who will proclaim the gospel to the distant lands of the Gentiles. The prophet says that Yahweh made this Messiah's "mouth like a sharp sword" (see Isaiah 49:2). While rulers thrive through violence, this coming Messiah will pierce the hearts and souls of his hearers with his words like a sharp sword.

In the Book of Nehemiah, when the people gather in the square, Ezra the priest brings the Book of the Law of Moses and reads it:

> **So Ezra the priest brought the Law before the assembly, both men and women and all who could understand what they heard, on the first day of the seventh month. And he read from it facing the square before the Water Gate from early morning until midday, in the presence of the men and the women and those who could understand. And the**

---

39   See Exodus 5:21, 15:9; Leviticus 26:7-8; Isaiah 3:25, ff.

**ears of all the people were attentive to the
Book of the Law.** NEHEMIAH 8:2-3

The end of such reading was that the people
understood God's Word (Nehemiah 8:8). The Word
of God, proclaimed like a two-edged sword, gave
understanding to God's people. Priests use this Spirit-
saturated sword to bring clarity to those who hear the
Word.

EMBRACING THE SWORD OF THE SPIRIT

We should read, study, live, and memorize the Word of
God. Any Christian who is even half-alert to his calling
understands that the Bible must play a crucial role in his
growth. But one of the significant problems of our day
is that we end up apologizing for the Bible more than
declaring its truths. We do not use it effectively, because
we view it selectively.

It is too common to act as if the Bible offers us a
choice of whether to take the Old or the New Testament.
It is embarrassing to see modern-day Christians publicly
discussing the Old Testament: they make absurd
bifurcations, acting as if the Bible is composed of a
mean God in the first thirty-nine books and a nice God
in the latter twenty-seven. The Church gives in to these
compromises when she fails to see the Word of God as
one story, inspired by the Holy Spirit.

Aaron was instructed to burn incense on the altar each morning and at twilight. These were regular offerings to Yahweh (Exodus 30:7-8), and God had a special recipe for this incense:

> The LORD said to Moses, "Take sweet spices, stacte, and onycha, and galbanum, sweet spices with pure frankincense (of each shall there be an equal part), and make an incense blended as by the perfumer, seasoned with salt, pure and holy. EXODUS 30:34-35

The altar of incense was called "Most Holy to the Lord." The incense was distinct from any other smell outside the sanctuary.

The Word of God is distinct from other incense. It has a unique flavor. Christians taste and see that the Lord is good, by tasting and seeing the Word of God. We treat it as most holy. It is a lamp unto our feet and light unto our paths. Like burning incense, we are to meditate on it day and night.

Imagine what would happen if the Church collectively said, "I trust the Word of God, even the parts that are difficult to understand."

What if, instead of putting the Word of God on trial, our hearts were on trial? Our actions on trial? Our anger, anxieties, and relationships on trial? Judged, delivered, and changed by the Word of God? It is remarkable that we often feel like we can lord it over God's word and act as if our feeble minds can determine what is valid and what is not.

In the Bible, when God spoke to his servants, there was no debate about whether it was God or not. When God spoke to Adam, Adam knew precisely who it was. When Yahweh spoke to Noah, Noah knew. When God asked Abraham to sacrifice his only son, Abraham did not once question whether or not it was God.

Yet when it comes to God's sword—which is the Word of God—we are suddenly having debates with ourselves. We despise the Devil, but deep inside, we too are saying, "Did God really say… ?" "Perhaps it was just a suggestion, not a command." At the end of every day, our sinful actions stem from viewing the sword of the Spirit as a flexible toy that blows with the wind.

Baptism gives entry into the armor of God, but what keeps us in the armor is our God-given ability to use the sword as intended.

When Samuel anointed David, the Spirit of the Lord came powerfully upon him (1 Samuel 16:13). The very next episode is the David and Goliath incident. We know the story well, but there is one detail that we often overlook. When David defeats Goliath, there is no reference to a sword in David's hands. Why? Because the Lord is David's sword. David says, "The Lord saves, not the sword."

But after David killed Goliath, what did he do? David ran and stood over him. He took hold of the Philistine's sword and drew it from the sheath. Having conquered his enemy, David cut off his head with the sword (1 Samuel 17:51).

The entire scene is dramatic and bloody. David sees an enemy who wants to desecrate the holy by destroying the holy priesthood of God—but no one is willing to move toward the enemy. They prefer to cower and allow the *enemy's* sword to attack *them*.

But David sees the holy as a Christian should, and like the angel, he will not allow evil to re-enter the sacred, to corrupt it. He takes the sword and cuts off the head of Goliath as a souvenir of God's grace. He takes the enemy's weapon and uses it to end evil by cutting off the head.

David moves forward with God's Word to destroy evil and everything that evil represents. Of course, the symbolism behind the cutting of the head is to fulfill the promise that the seed of the woman shall crush the head of the serpent.

At no point does David act in doubt concerning God's truth or his character. He moves with confidence. The Spirit is his priestly sword. He is anointed and baptized for this task. His helmet is on—which is to say that God's blessing is his, and David charges the gates of Hell rather than quietly waiting for the gates of Hell to charge him. The sword of the Spirit is ever pursuing to judge evil.

The Bible is a two-edged sword piercing and transforming whatever is not in conformity to its revelation. The Spirit's work convicts us of our sins and conforms us to the Word made flesh, Jesus Christ.

BELIEVE THE SWORD OF THE SPIRIT

We need more Bible readers, but this presupposes Bible believers. When you come to church to hear, confess, recite, and sing the Scriptures, come prepared to be changed by the Word of God. When you come to church, ask God that the service and the Word preached will minister to your heart in some way: challenging, changing, calling you to something new.

The Word does not come back void, but sometimes you make void the Word. You may sit Sunday after Sunday, hearing it preached. You may listen to the message repeatedly, yet nothing is different. You do not love your siblings or parents or spouse more, you are not praying more, you are not worshiping more, and you are not serving more.

What causes such complacency? Many Christians read or hear the Word but fail to believe it. We make the Word void in our hearts by treating it as a fine piece of literature rather than the living communication of God to us.

The way we use the divine Word explains our belief in the Word. Do you operate on a use-only-when-convenient paradigm? Are you acting like a politician in election year, when you pull out your favorite verse and turn it into a nice saying?

The sword of the Spirit is meant to move, causing things to change around us, turning evil into good and immorality into purity. Have you allowed the sacred to be constantly trespassed by evildoers? Images on your screen? Ungodly conversations and language? Bad influences that corrupt good morals?

Did you abandon the post in the garden, or are you using your sword to cause havoc on sin?

Put on the armor of God and be faithful to the little things in front of you. The sword of the Spirit will guide you to the Word of God, who is our belt, breastplate, shoes, shield, and helmet.

All six pieces are established in this armor; it is secure. But there is something Paul adds—not as a seventh armor piece, but as a final ritual to send armored men and women into the world.

THE BENEDICTION
OF THE ARMOR

....

Some things are very natural in the Christian life. But others require a lot of work—like loving people of whom you are not particularly fond, being interrupted to do something for the least of these, or standing for your faith on moral issues when it could cost you your job. We are called to be faithful in all these things, but they often do not come naturally.

The Bible spends much time exhorting us to love one another, encourage one another, sing to one another, restore one another, and so on. These commands imply that communion within the Body is fraught with difficulties.

Then, there is a category of practices that ought to be natural for the Christian. Praying is in that category. A spirit of prayerfulness should encompass the Christian. But for some reason, praying has become a problematic Christian exercise. "I will pray about it" has become synonymous with "Thanks for letting me know." It has become a cliché in our culture. Why? Because saying you are "praying" is an easy way out of any conversation. It also tends to separate yourself from the person and their story with one easy sentence.

If statistics are right, 14% of Evangelicals pray only once a week and 4% pray only once a month.[40] If you are in the 14%, that means that church is the only time in the week when you invest in self-conscious prayer. I hope we are in another bracket altogether, and pray daily and often.

The Apostle Paul expects a certain level of continuity in our prayer life. He commands us to "pray without ceasing" (1 Thessalonians 5:17). Now, at the end of his armor theology, Paul bathes every piece with prayer:

> **...Praying at all times in the Spirit, with all prayer and supplication. To that end, keep alert with all perseverance, making supplication for all the saints, and also for me, that words may be given to me in opening my mouth boldly to proclaim the mystery of the gospel, for which I am an ambassador in chains, that I may declare it boldly, as I ought to speak.**
>
> EPHESIANS 6:18-20

Paul has built his argument from the priestly garments of Aaron and his sons, and now it is clear that

---

40   https://www.pewforum.org/religious-landscape-study/frequency-of-prayer

he ends like Aaron does. He concludes the armor of God with a benediction.

Paul says, "praying at all times," and then he adds a prayer. The blessing upon armor-bearers is a priestly one, which harkens back to the famous Aaronic benediction in Numbers 6. It is a benediction used at the end of liturgical services in various traditions.

THE GREATER BENEDICTION

But before delving briefly into the prayer in Numbers 6, it is crucial to note that Jesus also ends with an Aaronic benediction as he ascends into the heavens. The disciples are examples of men who put on the armor, and valiantly—through many toils and snares—ended the race. Paul follows Christ's priestly pattern by pouring a benediction on his disciples.

At the end of Luke's Gospel, Jesus ends with priestly hands lifted up, blessing the disciples:

> **And he led them out as far as Bethany,**
> **and lifting up his hands he blessed them.**
> **While he blessed them, he parted from**
> **them and was carried up into heaven.**
>
> LUKE 24:50-51

This is Luke's conclusion to a lengthy argument that began in his first chapter. At the beginning of Luke, Mary was blessed because she believed the Lord would fulfill his promise to be faithful to Israel. Now, at the end of

Luke, the disciples received a blessing. Mary was blessed for believing, and now Jesus blesses all believers who trust Mary's God. The blessings are accumulated throughout Luke's narrative and reach a crescendo at the very end.

It is one thing to be blessed by Jesus before the Resurrection, but the Ascension blessing from Jesus is something even greater in magnitude, because the Ascension is the enthronement of Jesus at the right hand of the Father. He receives all authority in Heaven above and earth below, to commission the disciples to make more disciples, baptizing them in the Triune Name (Matthew 28:18-20). In the Ascension, Jesus seals his presence with them forever by offering a benediction.

This benediction is a magnificent fulfillment of many Old Testament promises. It is a build-up of the Aaronic benediction in Numbers 6 that we hear at the end of worship services. But there is an even more precise parallel in the Bible: it is found in Leviticus 9, when Aaron blesses the people and then offers a sacrifice of sin offering, burnt offering, and fellowship offering. Sin offering refers to the absolution of sins, burnt offering (literally "ascension offering") is a gift that goes up into the heavens, and fellowship offering is a gift of restored communion.

Aaron blesses the people and restores them to God's presence by offering atonement on their behalf. Aaron prays for the forgiveness of sins, and that God would bestow peace upon them. Remember how the priestly benediction goes:

> The LORD bless you and keep you; the LORD make his face to shine upon you and be gracious to you; the LORD lift up his countenance upon you and give you peace. NUMBERS 6:24-26

Did Aaron's benediction provide for the people in every way? The blessing did provide wisdom and courage for God's people in the Old Covenant. But when Aaron blessed the people as a priest, he could not provide the full wisdom of the counsel of God or the unhindered courage for God's people to fight against the schemes of the devil. Aaron's benediction did not fully bless or fully keep; Yahweh's face did not shine fully, nor could he be fully gracious or lift up his countenance to grant them full peace.

It is not because God was incapable of doing these things, but because God was only revealed fully to his people when in the fullness of time came (Galatians 4:4).

When Jesus lifts his hands to bless the disciples, he is blessing them the way the Israelites were intended to be blessed. He can grant them peace because they have seen God's face in Christ and experienced the keeping and guarding ministry of Jesus for three years. The greater Aaron lifted them up from despair and doubt, and now they have tasted the glory of God in him. Aaron could not fully bless them, but Jesus blesses to the uttermost as the great and final High Priest.

This blessing that Jesus offers before the Ascension is the ultimate priestly blessing, the fulfillment of all blessings, the full and the vindicated smile of God upon his children. Aaron offered a benediction in the absence of the God-Man, but the God-Man, the Great Priest, offers himself as a benediction to us.

And because Jesus is the embodied benediction of the Father, he now says, "You will be my ambassadors of blessing as I rule and reign at the right hand of the Father." The armor you wear is full of grace and truth.

THE PAULINE BENEDICTION

The armor of God is Christ's gift to the Church, sealed in this Ascension benediction.

> **Therefore it says, "When he ascended on high he led a host of captives, and he gave gifts to men."** EPHESIANS 4:8

In the Ascension, Paul says, Christ obtained victory over death and gave gifts to his Church. This is why Paul ends Ephesians with the finest gift—the gift of putting on Christ. Christ conquered death and Hell; so now we fight against death and Hell.

Paul gives us a parting prayer. This was in contrast to the religious leaders of the first century, who prayed in a way that God despised. They were self-righteous about their prayers. They did not pour God's favor upon the people, but the law's curses.

In contrast, the royal priesthood prays at all times in the Spirit. They pray over one another, indwelt by the Spirit of God, who helps us in our weakness and intercedes for us with groanings too deep for words. When our faith is too small to receive the blessings of God over our armor, the Spirit intercedes for the saints according to the will of God (Romans 8:26-27).

Paul says that to pray in the Spirit requires alertness and perseverance, as we pray for the saints and those in positions of leadership:

> **To that end, keep alert with all perseverance...** EPHESIANS 6:18b

One of the repeated themes throughout this book is that wearing the armor of God implies that we are constantly warring against principalities and powers— that there are forces greater than ourselves which we cannot control.

So, following the discourse about the armor, Paul enters this conversation about prayer. These are not separate things. He says that since the armor is Spirit-led, so is our prayer. The armor of God must be sealed in the priestly benedictions for it to function according to God's promises. If we remove the prayer of the saints, we have an unblessed armor. The Christian armor must be strengthened by prayer.

Prayer is pneumatological, Spirit-oriented and directed. In the Bible, the Spirit hovers over all Creation, and over the direct rulers in Israel's history. The Holy Spirit keeps the Church united in 1 Corinthians, prays for us in Romans, and calls us to the throne of grace in Revelation. From beginning to end, the Spirit christens our armor with his presence.

Prayer is participation in the life of the Spirit. We could say the Triune life of the Spirit, but for Paul, prayer is to be particularly "in the Spirit." To have a fully Trinitarian life, we need a life of prayer. Perhaps one reason we think so rarely about the role of the Spirit is that we are not continually abiding in the presence of the Spirit in prayer.

So, if this is how we participate in the life of the Spirit, it would be wise to be in the Spirit as we walk together, fighting against principalities and powers.

HOW TO PRAY?

Prayer can often be too abstract in our war against evil. I hope you would understand more fully how Christ blesses us by the power of the Spirit. But sometimes, we do not know how to pray.

Here are a few principles to remember as you ask for God's blessings upon the armor.

■ PRAY MEANINGFULLY

Sometimes we fear anything formal or written, but our prayers become more meaningful when we think about what to pray and frequently practice prayer. We are not required to use more theological words, but to be more *meaningful* in our communion with God. We often find ourselves caught off guard when someone calls us to pray. Part of our problem is that we are comfortable being amateurs at praying.

Sinclair Ferguson put it this way:

> *You do not become a master musician by playing just as you please, by imagining that learning the scales is sheer legalism and bondage! No, true freedom in any area of life is the consequence of regular discipline. It is no less true of the life of prayer.*[41]

We do not want to practice prayer because we do not want to develop prayer. As a result, we find ourselves unequipped to pray more faithfully. Prayer requires practice.

Jesus condemns the vain repetition of the Pharisees because there is a kind of vain repetition that is self-serving, but what about the casual vain repetition we do when we refuse to learn how to be meaningful and intentional in our prayer?

....

41 Sinclair Ferguson, *Grow in Grace* (Carlisle, PA: Banner of Truth, 1989), p. 105.

■ PRAY COMMUNALLY

Praying together helps us to learn from one another how to pray better, and it also helps us share our burdens with one another. We often don't know what to pray because we are not in close communion with brothers and sisters to understand their needs.

If every time someone says, "Pray for me," we stopped and prayed for them, we would have a much more pleasant experience in our prayer life, and we would embody Paul's words to "pray continually."

■ PRAY HISTORICALLY

The Spirit prolongs the life of ideas throughout history. The reason Augustine, Calvin, and Luther changed the course of history for the good is because the Spirit used these men's ideas to change the direction of the Church.

In some ways, we have made prayer so informal that we have forgotten our history of prayer. I know we may not always have the time to write or read those prayers written by the Church, but I would encourage you to consider these prayers not as the ideal, but as guides—in the drive to church, before lunch, or before a business meeting. Perhaps, with every three to four prayers you do, spontaneously use something historical in addition. You can use it at the dinner table or any other environment, and you will be quickly surprised at just how many prayers have been written for virtually every occasion.

As G.K. Chesterton says,

> *You say grace before meals. All right. But*
> *I say grace before the concert and the opera,*
> *and grace before the play and pantomime,*
> *and grace before I open a book, and grace*
> *before sketching, painting, swimming,*
> *fencing, boxing, walking, playing, dancing*
> *and grace before I dip the pen in the ink.*[42]

Prayer is normal. But like most ordinary things in our Christian lives, we need to nurture this practice. I pray that God would instill in us an urgency to pray, not just as a necessary duty of words, but as an essential duty of godly wisdom. After all, if we are to put on the armor of God, each piece must be bathed in prayers in and through the power of the Spirit.

....

42 https://www.chesterton.org/quotations/essential-chesterton

DR. URIESOU BRITO is the Senior Pastor of Providence Church (CREC) in Pensacola, Florida. As an editor and author, he has many publications to his name, including *The Church-Friendly Family*, *The Trinitarian Father*, *An Introduction to Holy Incense*, and commentaries on Ruth and Jonah. He writes for various magazines and websites, including the *Journal of Religious Leadership*, Theopolis blog, and *Fight Laugh Feast* magazine. He founded Kuyperian Commentary, an online resource for essays and podcasts with over 20 contributors, and hosts the *Perspectivalist* podcast. Learn more at **uribrito.com**.